FLOATING KITCHENS
Cooking with Seattle's Houseboaters

Floating Homes Association
Seattle, Washington

All profits derived from sales of *Floating Kitchens* will be used to support the purpose and programs of the
Floating Homes Association.

To order additional copies of Floating Kitchens, please use the form provided in the back of this book.

Library of Congress Catalog Card Number 93-73967

ISBN 0-917656-20-2

Designed and produced by Marty Alexander and Ann Bassetti

Front cover artwork by Elissa Kamins

Chapter divider page illustrations by Peg Boley

Back cover photograph by Phil H. Webber

Other illustrations by Peg Boley, Elissa Kamins and Beth Means

Printed on recycled paper (20% post-consumer waste)

TABLE OF CONTENTS

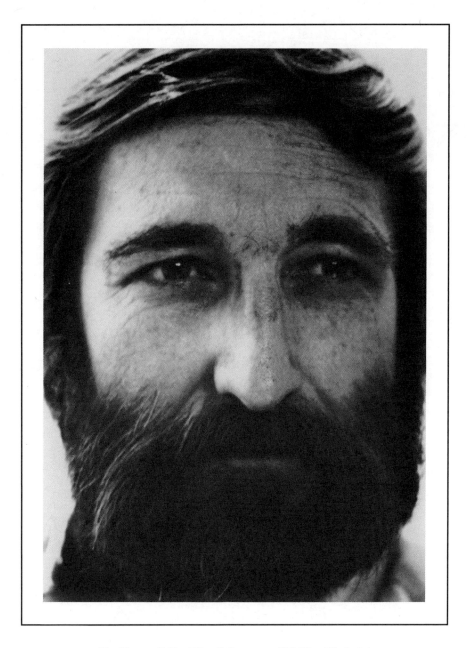

Dedicated To The Memory Of Jim Knight

During the legal battles to save our houseboats and the fight for an Equity Ordinance, the Floating Homes Association incurred tens of thousands of dollars in expenses. In 1981, a Fund Raising Committee was formed with Jim at the helm. With his guidance, encouragement and great "down home" sense of humor we were able to raise the much-needed dollars — beginning with a Pete Seeger concert, followed by numerous houseboat tours and auctions. We couldn't have done it without him.

Acknowledgments

The Floating Homes Association thanks our members, their families and friends who have contributed recipes and anecdotes for this cookbook.

Special thanks to the people who generously donated countless hours of their time to produce this cookbook: Marty Alexander, Ann Bassetti, Peg Boley, June Fauchald, Becky Foley, Marty Gardner, Sheri Gotay, Elissa Kamins, Nancy MacDonald, Jann McFarland, Beth Means, Tom and Peg Stockley, Phil Webber.

THE FLOATING HOMES ASSOCIATION

Houseboats are as old as Seattle. The first were built to house the workers at logging camps. In the 1920's, more appeared as summer homes on Lake Washington and homes for fishermen, boat builders, and others along the waterways. Most of today's houseboats were built in the 1930's as "temporary" cheap housing during the Great Depression. By the 1940's there were over 2,000, and the community was a lively mix of students, artists, and modest blue and pink collar working people.

Declaring Lake Union to be the "cesspool of Seattle", the City fathers launched an all-out campaign in the 1950's to rid the City of houseboats. They banned houseboats on Lake Washington, then zoned the remaining houseboat docks for apartments and offices, targeted government projects at existing docks, drew construction limit lines through the middle of existing docks (and then threatened to throw everyone over the line off), and finally adopted restrictions on new houseboat docks that made it impossible to develop any new docks for displaced houseboats. By the early 1960's, only 1,000 houseboats remained and new ordinances loomed declaring houseboats a public health hazard.

In 1962 the Floating Homes Association was formed. Declaring its mission "to protect Seattle's old and colorful houseboat colony" the Association began to fight back, starting with a plan to hook every houseboat to the city sewer system — no small engineering feat — as a counter to the public health ordinances. Since then the Association has fought to replace the "scorched earth" apartment zoning with protective single family zoning, a goal partially achieved in the mid-1980's. The houseboats are now down to 487 (and holding!) and the Association tries to find moorage for any displaced houseboat. We are still working to have construction limit lines recognize historic docks. We continue to encourage Metro to separate storm and sanitary sewers so that the City stops dumping sewage into Lake Union.

In the 1970's a new, unforeseen issue loomed. The accumulated restrictions had the effect of giving dock owners a virtual monopoly on each houseboat space. In 1975 the first houseboat evicted from its moorage was sold as scrap wood for want of a legal moorage. Some dock owners began abusing their monopoly, and the houseboat wars were back in the papers again.

The Floating Homes Association responded by proposing the "Floating Homes Equity Ordinance," the first of its kind, to regulate the monopoly. Thirty homeowners threatened with eviction by 3 dock owners filed an anti-trust suit. After a couple of attempts, an Equity Ordinance acceptable to the State Supreme Court was ultimately adopted and is now used as a model by houseboaters all over the world. The anti-trust suit was settled out of court, and the Association launched a campaign to help all houseboaters form cooperatives to buy their docks or to get long term leases — a project that continues to this day.

The Lake is quiet today, but houseboaters know it's an uneasy calm and many of the elements of the houseboat extermination plan still remain to be changed. After its thirty year battle to save the houseboats, the Floating Homes Association has learned to stand ready at the helm with an eye on the horizon for the next storm.

Beth Means

WHEN FRIENDS FLOAT BY

Appetizers

FATAL FETA

1 lb. imported Greek feta cheese
1/2 cup cottage cheese
1/3 cup (approximately) plain yogurt
6 to 10 cloves garlic, medium size
3 T. olive oil

Makes 1 medium bowl of dip.

In a wide bowl, coarsely grate feta cheese and add cottage cheese, yogurt, garlic cloves (crushed) and olive oil. Stir thoroughly and refrigerate 4 to 24 hours before serving. Serve with crusty white bread chunks or "toasties" (small diameter French bread loaves sliced, then toasted lightly, like chips).

Note: A food processor works great for crumbling the cheese and mincing the garlic, but you should hand mix the dip itself to retain texture.

Art Hemenway

This stuff is lethal — everyone has to participate or they will be gasping for air amid the clouds of garlic produced by this dip! Don't eat it before a big meeting, job interview, etc.

DOCKAMOLE

2 large ripe avocados (at least)
2 T. cream cheese
2 T. salsa
1 tsp. mayonnaise
1 tsp. sour cream
1 ripe tomato, chopped
Garlic salt

Makes about 2 1/2 cups.

Peel and smash avocados. Add about 2 T. cream cheese and continue pulverizing. Stir in some salsa (about 2 T.). Add mayonnaise and sour cream. Toss in chopped tomato. Sprinkle in some garlic salt (be generous) and stir until all ingredients are well blended.

Pam & Dave Sanford

Passed down through every generation of Sanford males for hundreds of years.

UP-FOR-AUCTION CLAM AND CHEESE CANAPÉS

This recipe was used as part of a catering package sold at a Floating Homes Auction.

1 cup grated cheddar cheese
1 8 oz. can minced clams, drained
Pinch of cayenne pepper
2 T. chopped parsley
1 T. chopped chives (optional)
Toast Rounds

Makes at least 16, usually more.

Combine cheese, clams and seasonings. Spread on toast rounds and slip under preheated broiler until cheese melts.

Ellen Hansen

PROSCIUTTO & APPLES

1/4 lb. very thinly sliced Italian prosciutto
2-3 tart apples
Juice of 1 lemon
Cracked black pepper

Makes 3-4 dozen slices.

Halve and core the apples and slice into wedges about 1/2" wide at the skin. Toss gently in a bowl with the lemon juice to prevent discoloration. Drain and allow to dry a bit.

Gently peel a slice of prosciutto from the rest and cut in half lengthwise. Wrap around a slice of apple and place on a serving plate. When all are done, grind a little cracked black pepper over the top.

As a variation, spread a small amount of cream cheese or montrachet on the side of the apple before wrapping with prosciutto.

Diane Pettengill from Ladies Poker Night

Losing at poker isn't so bad when you can console yourself with treats like this.

A *"floating home", "houseboat",
or, sometimes , "boathouse" in
Seattle is a regular (permanent,
year-round) house built on a log
raft, though the newer ones are
sometimes built on rafts of cement
and styrofoam. There are 487 of
them, all found on Lake Union or
Portage Bay. Houseboats can be
seen in Seattle, Vancouver
(Washington and Canada), San
Francisco Bay (in Sausalito), across
from Atlantic City, London,
Amsterdam, and maybe
elsewhere too.*

Beth Means

ARTICHOKE DIP

1 large can artichokes, drained and chopped
1 can (4 oz.) chopped green chiles
1/2 cup grated Parmesan cheese
1/2 cup Best Foods Real Mayonnaise (not Light)

Serves 4-6.

Mix ingredients and microwave to heat through. Serve with crackers or corn chips or in a hollowed-out sour dough loaf.

Joan Hacker

ANNUAL MT. ST. HELENS/DOCK BUYING MEMORIAL PARTY MUNCHIES

1 8-oz. package of Philadelphia cream cheese
1/4 tsp. paprika
1/4 tsp. garlic salt
3/4 tsp. dill weed

Makes 1 cup.

Mash the paprika, garlic salt, and dill weed into the cream cheese until well mixed (the paprika will turn the spread a light salmon color). Spread on Waverly Wafers or other sturdy crackers.

Sheri Lockwood

Our "Dox" first annual party coincided with the May 18, 1980, eruption of Mt. St. Helens. So we have a party in our parking lot every year to commemorate the volcano and the sometimes volcanic process of buying our dock. "Dox" is the name of our cooperatively owned moorage consisting of 31 houseboats tied up to 2 docks.

Our monthly Ladies Poker Night has been going on for nearly three years now. Some traditions have developed. For instance, the first time a new person is invited she always says she doesn't know how to play and proceeds to take all our money. The only person to ever get a natural royal flush was never asked back. If you stick with it through your losing streak (months) your luck will eventually change.

Don't gloat too much — bad karma. Cackling as you rake in the chips is OK. When you deal your own favorite game, you lose. When you play your least favorite game, you win. Some of us like straight poker and some of us call 3 or 4 wild cards. Zen (no peekee) is one of our favorites.

(cont'd next page)

CROSTINI À LA POKER

1 loaf crusty Italian bread
1/4 cup olio santo (1/4 cup olive oil, crushed red pepper, crushed garlic)
Chèvre (goat cheese)
2 heads roasted garlic
1 roasted red bell pepper

Serves 6-8.

Slice and lightly toast bread. Spread each slice with oil and 1 or 2 cloves of roasted garlic, chèvre, and top with a few slices of roasted pepper. Lightly brown under the broiler and serve.

Marney Reynolds from Ladies Poker Night

Smoked Cod Spread

1/2 lb. smoked black cod or other good smoked fish
Softened cream cheese (3 oz. pkg. or to taste)
Dollop of mayonnaise
Chives, chopped fine
Herb toast or cherry tomatoes

Serves 4-6.

Cream ingredients gently together. Spread on herb toasts or stuff into cherry tomatoes.

Diane Pettengill from Ladies Poker Night

This monthly game has seen us through being dumped, being the dumper, moving, getting married, buying houses, self-doubts, celebrations, aging, unemployment, self-employment, babies, the non-committal guy, being non-committal. Through each other's eyes, we've seen it all. We still get pretty rowdy so we warn our houseboat neighbors ahead of time. At a nickel ante we can lose our shirts and still get off cheaper than going to a movie. And Ladies Poker Night has one definite advantage over guys poker night — GREAT FOOD!

Sheri Lockwood

*M*ost older houseboats are built
on log rafts. Large 6" x 8" timbers,
called "stringers", are laid on top of
the raft, and the house is built on
the stringers. Periodically these
stringers rot away and must be
replaced, a messy job involving
jacking up the house on old water-
filled fire hoses, pulling out the old
stringers and pushing in the new
ones. It used to be done barn-
raising style with all the neighbors
helping and was an excuse for a
dock potluck party as well.

Beth Means

SESAME CHICKEN

1 T. vegetable oil
1 small clove garlic, minced
4 chicken breasts, skinned, boned and cut into 1" cubes
2 T. soy sauce
3 T. firmly packed brown sugar
1/2 tsp. ground ginger
3 T. toasted sesame seeds

Serves 6-8.

Heat the oil in a heavy skillet. Add the garlic and chicken. Sauté over high heat for 3 minutes or until chicken is about half cooked.

Combine the soy sauce, sugar and ginger. Add to the chicken and continue to sauté over high heat until most of the liquid is evaporated and the chicken is glazed, about 4 minutes.

Remove from heat and chill. Sprinkle with the sesame seeds and toss before serving. Serve with toothpicks.

C.J. Eriksen

ROASTED GARLIC

8 heads fresh garlic
1/2 cup olive oil
1/4 cup butter (melted)
1/4 cup water
1/4 lb. goat cheese (montrachet, chèvre) thinly sliced or
   crumbled
Herbs: Any of rosemary, basil, oregano or thyme

Serves 4-6.

Preheat oven to 275 F.

Peel loose paper off garlic heads but leave cloves intact in casing. Cut
1/4 inch off top of each head of garlic (not root end). Put in oven-proof
pan just large enough to hold garlic, cut side up. Pour olive oil, butter
and water over garlic. Season with herbs.

Cover pan tightly with foil. Bake two hours or until garlic is very soft
and spreadable.

Take individual garlic cloves, squeeze out and spread on toast rounds.
Top with goat cheese.

Marty Gardner

We houseboaters revel in summer. Because houseboats are generally fairly small, summer means we can desert tiny kitchens and living rooms and move to the wide open spaces of the deck for salads, barbecues and light dinners. From the deck, we can watch our neighbors mosey up and down the dock (to which our houses are tied to keep them from floating away — also providing phone service, water, sewer lines, electricity and access to shore), and visit with passing ducks, geese, boaters and swimmers. If we want a cooling dip before dinner we've only to jump off the porch. If we forgot to go shopping, we just jump onto someone else's deck when we know the burgers are done.

Beth Means

*From 1939 to 1942 my grandmother, Stella Anderson, lived on a houseboat over by the locks, on the south side of the channel. My father helped her out by rowing across to Ballard to get her groceries. In 1959 I bought an old houseboat for $1400. The moorage fees were $25, including water and garbage. It sounds inexpensive now, but remember that I only made $99/month in those days. I sold the house in 1962 — probably at a loss — because I couldn't afford to pay to have it hooked up to the city sewer. **Gary Seese**

BLUE CHEESE GOO

1/4 cup diet sour cream
1/2 stick of softened low fat cream cheese
1/4 cup plain yogurt
Blue, roquefort or gorgonzola cheese, crumbled (to taste)
Splash white wine vinegar

Makes about 1 cup.

Cream sour cream, cream cheese and yogurt together. Add vinegar and mix. Gently stir in blue, roquefort or gorgonzola cheese. Serve with "Finger Fries" (below), vegetables, or BBQ chicken wings.

FINGER FRIES

2 or 3 medium russet potatoes
Olive oil
Ground cayenne pepper
Paprika
Garlic powder
Fresh parsley or chives, chopped

Serves 4-6.

Scrub potatoes and slice into wedges lengthwise. Try to cut them so they will stand up with the skin side down. Pat dry and brush with olive oil. Arrange them on a large cookie sheet, leaving a little space between the slices. Sprinkle with the spices, starting with the cayenne so you can see how much you use.

Bake in preheated 425 F. oven for 30-40 minutes or until golden brown. Transfer to a platter, garnish with chopped parsley or chives, and serve with "Blue Cheese Goo" (above) or boring old catsup.

Diane Pettengill from Ladies Poker Night

ARTICHOKE NIBBLES

3 jars (6-oz.) marinated artichoke hearts
1 medium onion, finely chopped
1 1/2 garlic cloves, minced
6 eggs, beaten
1/2 cup fine bread crumbs
1/4 tsp. salt, pepper, and oregano
1/4 tsp. Tabasco
3 cups shredded sharp cheddar cheese
3 T. fresh parsley, minced

Serves 10-15.

Drain marinade from 1/2 the artichokes into skillet; drain remaining marinade and discard. Chop artichokes and set aside. Heat marinade oil, add onion and garlic and sauté. In a bowl, combine eggs, bread crumbs, seasonings, and Tabasco. Fold in the cheese and parsley. Add the artichokes and the sautéed onion mixture. Blend well.

Bake in a 9" x 13" baking dish in a 325 F. oven approximately 30 minutes. Cool briefly and cut into 1" squares.

Kendall

My friend Sarah brought this as an hors d'oeuvre to a New Year's Eve party, and it has been a potluck favorite ever since.

SPICY PEANUT DIP

This dip is great with cool, crunchy vegetables like celery, cucumbers, sugar peas, lightly cooked green beans and broccoli.

1/2 cup peanut butter
Fresh lemon juice
Thai chile paste, to taste
2 T. sour cream
Splash rice wine vinegar

Makes about 3/4 cup.

Mix all ingredients together. Consistency is controlled by amount of liquid you choose to add. "Heat", of course, depends on how courageous you are with the chile paste. Tabasco may be used, but it is not the same.

Diane Pettengill from Ladies Poker Night

STUFFED MUSHROOMS

1 lb. medium fresh mushrooms
6 T. butter
1/2 cup chopped onions
1 cup soft bread crumbs
1 cup shredded cheddar cheese
1/4 cup chopped parsley
1/2 tsp. salt
1/2 tsp. black pepper

Serves 8.

Rinse, pat dry and remove stems from mushrooms. Chop stems (makes
about 1 1/2 cups) and set aside. In a large skillet, melt butter. Brush
mushroom caps with butter and place in a shallow baking dish. Sauté
onions and chopped mushroom stems in butter for about 2 minutes.
Then add bread crumbs, cheese, parsley, salt and pepper and stir lightly.
Spoon mixture into mushroom caps. Bake at 350 F. until hot, about 20
minutes. Serve immediately.

Pat Swain

We made a big batch of this for an "After the Pete Seeger Concert" party, and we ended up dunking kazoos in the dip and blowing bubbles and kazooing through the dip. For those who weren't there, Pete Seeger came to Seattle and gave a wonderful benefit concert for the Floating Homes Assocation, honoring Terry Pettus the day the Mayor declared Terry "Citizen of the Year". Terry Pettus was Executive Secretary of the Floating Homes Association for over 15 years and adopted grandfather to many of us houseboaters. He led the fight to save Seattle's houseboat community from abolition favored by the City and in the process saved Lake Union itself as a thriving, working lake.

KAZOO CON QUESO DIP

2 8-oz. pkgs. cream cheese
1 can tomatoes and green chiles or
    1 8-oz. can whole tomatoes and
    1 small can chopped green chiles
Hot sauce to taste

Makes 1 large bowl (suitable for 26 kazoos)

Cook all ingredients over low heat until cheese is melted and ingredients are well mixed and smooth. Serve in chafing dish or fondue pot with homemade tortilla chips.

Jann McFarland

SEASONED OYSTER CRACKERS

1 box or pkg. oyster crackers (approx. 12 oz.)
1 pkg. Hidden Valley Ranch salad dressing mix
  ("Buttermilk Original Recipe")
3/4-1 cup salad oil
1/2 tsp. lemon pepper
1/2 tsp. dill weed
1/2 tsp. garlic powder (or more)
1/4 tsp. onion powder
1/4 tsp. cayenne pepper

These are good! Bet you can't eat just one. Can be served with soups, or just as a snack. Given to me by the best cook in Kerrville, Texas.

Spread crackers in cake pan or cookie sheet with sides (so they won't slide off). Combine dry Hidden Valley Ranch salad dressing mix and salad oil. Add seasoning and pour over crackers. Toss a bit to coat crackers. Toast in 250 F. oven for about 45 minutes, stirring occasionally. Remove from oven and sprinkle on more seasoning to taste.

Dump on paper towels to absorb excess oil, if any. Will stay fresh in air tight container, or put them back in the oven to crisp them up.

Marty Gardner

TEXAS TRASH

1 pkg. long pretzels
1/2 box Cheerios
1 box Wheat Chex
1 box Rice Chex
1 lb. pecan halves
1 tsp. savory salt
1 stick margarine
3/4 cup bacon fat
2 T. Tabasco
1 1/2 tsp. garlic salt
2 T. liquid smoke
1 T. Worcestershire sauce

Makes lots!

Mix first 5 ingredients. Melt margarine and bacon fat. Add all liquids and spices. Pour over dry ingredients, coating well. Bake 1 hour at 250 F. Stir every 15 minutes.

Nancy MacDonald

Not for cholesterol counters!

'Nough Nachos

1 large pkg. corn chips (San Juan Salsa Co. is my favorite)
3-5 green onions, chopped
1/2 - 1 whole green, red, yellow, and/or jalapeno pepper,
    chopped
1 1/2 cups sharp cheddar cheese, grated

Serves 4-6.

Spread corn chips on a cookie sheet or oven-proof plate. Sprinkle with onions, peppers and cheese. Heat 5-8 minutes in 300 F. oven until the cheese is melted. Serve with fresh salsa laced with avocado.

Jeri Callahan

When you move into 300 square feet of houseboat, you have to make some basic decisions about entertaining. The first: "Can I?" From a well-supplied suburban kitchen I culled out two items for company. One is a cheese and cracker tray, the other a large oven-proof chop plate. The chop plate provides nachos for all sorts of occasions from dock potlucks to entertaining my most distinguished visitor, the Episcopal Bishop of Mexico City! Quantities are flexible, depending on the size of the crowd. This is a basic recipe. For "formal" occasions you can make it more of a meal by adding refried beans, fried Walla Walla sweets, ripe olives, sour cream and whatever else you find in your refrigerator. Like soup, nachos are no place for dogmatism!

CEVICHE

3 lbs. red snapper fillets
1 cup fresh lime juice
1/2 cup cider vinegar
1 onion, sliced
3 garlic cloves, sliced
1 T. salt
1/3 cup olive oil
3 or 4 drops of Tabasco

Serves 12 as appetizer.

Cut fillets in small cubes about 3/4". Marinate overnight in lime juice. In the morning add the rest of the ingredients after mixing. Leave in marinade several hours. Can be left several days without harm. Drain and serve with toothpicks.

Melinda Steinborn

This is a Steinborn family recipe. While they're not houseboaters, they're Lake Washingtoners from way back and have spent a lot of time in, on, under and around the water.

HOT CRAB DIP

2 pkgs. (8 oz. each) cream cheese, cubed
2 cans (6.5 oz. each) crab meat, drained
1 clove garlic, minced
1/2 cup mayonnaise
2 tsp. prepared mustard
1/4 cup sherry
1 T. minced onion
Seasoned salt to taste

Serves 8.

Combine all ingredients in a sauce pan. Heat until cheese is melted and sauce is smooth, stirring occasionally. Serve in chafing dish with crackers or very thin slices of French bread.

Joan Hacker

*C*ats are common on houseboat docks. Our dock once had 14 cats, all vying for territory. Felicia, the old grande dame, was struggling to hold off Minnesota Max, a new interloper. The situation finally came to a head as they leapt at each other from their opposing decks. They met mid-air, all claws, fangs and howls. But, in the heat of the moment, they had forgotten the watery chasm between them. Ker-splash! All was promptly forgotten in the scramble to get out of the water.

Shirley Thomas

*T*he houseboat at the end of a Fairview Avenue dock was ours for two weeks while its owners vacationed in Hawaii. On our third night, fierce winds powered a driving rainstorm out of the west. The houseboat heaved, creaked and groaned in the howling wind. I woke at the moment of impact. As the house lifted out of the water, glass and timber shattered and exploded and nails pulled free with ghastly shrieks. I reached for a light switch. A torrent of water gushed from the lighted fixture at the center of the twisting ceiling until a short extinguished it; sparks arced from circuits in and outside the house. Darkness. We were naked in a drenched bed, drapes and blinds flapped wildly, the piano slid towards the kitchen, shards of

(cont'd next page)

SUN-DRIED TOMATO BRUCHETTA

1 cup sun-dried tomatoes, dry
2 cups water
4 cloves garlic, whole
1/2 cup fresh Italian broadleaf parsley
1/2 cup fresh basil
3 tsp. dried oregano
2 T. olive oil
1 small sweet onion, quartered
Lots of cracked black pepper
1 baguette rustic Italian bread
Parmesan cheese, grated

Serves 8-10.

Place sun-dried tomatoes in sauce pan and pour water over. Bring to a boil, cover, and turn off heat. Let stand for 1/2 hour.

Drain the tomatoes (save broth for soup stock) and place in a food processor with the garlic, parsley, basil, oregano, olive oil, onion and pepper. Process until blended. Slice baguette into thin disks.

Preheat oven to 375 F. Lightly oil a cookie sheet and arrange the bread disks on it. Spread the tomato puree over each disk and sprinkle with Parmesan cheese. Bake for 10 minutes (or until Parmesan is melted) and serve.

Blair Robbins and Bob Burk

PICO DE GALLO

2 avocados
1/4 red bell pepper
1/4 yellow bell pepper
3-4 fresh tomatillos
1 small Roma tomato
1/2 medium size onion
3-4 fresh jalapeno peppers (or to taste)
2 T. fresh parsley
Juice of 1/2 lime
Salt and pepper

Serves 4 as an appetizer.

Cut up avocados, red and yellow peppers, tomatillos and tomato into half inch cubes (or smaller). Mince onion, jalapenos and parsley. Toss in a bowl. Add lime juice, salt and pepper to taste, and toss again. Let mixture sit for at least 30 minutes to mingle flavors. Serve with tortilla chips and margaritas.

Jann McFarland

glass everywhere, power lines sizzled and snapped on the dock. Was the houseboat moored or free? Floating or sinking? We managed to dress and climb through debris to safety. From the dock we could see what had happened: the wind had lifted the roof of the west-facing porch like a kite. But the roof could carry the house's weight out of water only so far before some-thing had to give — the roof had peeled back like the lid of a sardine can. At 4:40 a.m., we called and woke the owners in Hawaii. "You know your houseboat? . . . we began.

Dick Birnbaum

Keeping Warm On Stormy Seas

Soups and Sauces

HELEN'S FAMED BLACK BEAN SOUP

1 lb. black beans*
2 ribs celery, chopped
1 medium onion, chopped
1 ham bone or 1 cup small ham pieces
Juice of 2 lemons
1/2 tsp. dry Coleman's mustard
Garlic salt, salt, pepper, cayenne and Tabasco to taste
1/2 cup dry sherry
1 cup cooked white rice
1/2 cup grated or chopped onion

*T*his recipe dates from 1870 and is
one of my old standbys.

Serves 6.

Wash and soak black beans overnight. Drain. Add 2 quarts cold water, onion, celery and ham. Simmer 3 to 4 hours until beans are very tender. Remove ham bone; put all through blender. Add mustard, lemon, garlic salt, and see if you don't want a touch of Tabasco, too. Add salt, pepper and a pinch of cayenne. Simmer 30 minutes, then add 1/2 cup dry sherry and serve topped with a spoonful of fluffy white rice and a tsp. grated or chopped onion if desired.

*Be sure to get the tender kind of beans — gourmet departments often have them in fancy boxes and these are fine.

Helen Mitchell

SOUR MUSHROOM SOUP

1/4 lb. dried mushrooms
1 1/2 quarts water
Sauerkraut juice from 1 large can of sauerkraut
1 clove garlic, whole
Salt and pepper to taste
1/2 cup orzo pasta (#47 Ronzoni)
2-4 T. oil
2-4 T. flour

Serves 6-8.

Soak mushrooms for 30 minutes in 2 cups of cold water. Remove from water and cut into small pieces. Strain the mushroom juice through cheesecloth and add 1 1/2 quarts of water to it. Squeeze the sauerkraut until dry to extract all juice. Add cut up mushrooms, garlic clove and sauerkraut juice, salt and pepper to water. Cook about 1 1/2 hours over low heat. Remove garlic clove. More sauerkraut juice can be added to make it more sour. Add uncooked pasta.

In a small frying pan add oil and flour, stir constantly until brown. Add to soup and cook until thickened.

Susan Chatlos-Susor

This is a Chatlos family Christmas Eve tradition to start the old Ukrainian-Polish holiday dinner. Mom makes this for about 23 people, so it's a family effort to save up enough sauerkraut juice for her to make it in that great a quantity!

GRANDMA MARY'S HUNGARIAN RIND SOUPPE DINNER

2 to 3 lbs. ox tails
6 small boiling onions
6 small potatoes
6 small carrots
1 lb. parsnips
1/2 tsp. (1/4 oz.) fresh parsley
6 to 12 peppercorns
Dash cayenne
1 bay leaf
1/8 oz. (1 pkg.) saffron
1 T. Hungarian paprika (or to taste)
Salt to taste

Fresh noodles :
1 1/2 cups all-purpose flour
3/4 tsp. salt
2 eggs
2 tsp. cooking oil
2 tsp. water

This recipe was served to me often by my Grandma Mary Wespecher who came from a German settlement in Hungary. She also had some Swiss blood. Hungarians are a very mixed bunch of folks like the houseboat community. It was usually served to me after I mowed her lawn and picked apples on Saturday afternoons. While I was working, she was cooking. I used to sneak in every once in a while to watch her make those noodles!

Serves 4.

Crack ox tails if you wish. Put them in a pot and pour in just enough cold water to cover them. Simmer for 3 hours or until meat begins to fall off the bone. Tie parsley and peppercorns in cheesecloth bag and add to pot along with potatoes and onions. Cook on medium heat for another 15 minutes. Add parsnips, carrots, salt, cayenne and bay leaf. Simmer an additional 20 minutes or less so parsnips do not become too soft. Remove from heat. Strain broth into a separate saucepan and bring to a boil. Add noodles to boiling broth and boil for 3 minutes. Add paprika and saffron. Cook on low heat 5 minutes more. Serve soup separately from meat and vegetables.

Noodles: Combine flour and salt in mixing bowl. Make a well in the center. Beat eggs, oil and water together; pour into well. Stir with fork from outside of mixture to center. Add a little water so a stiff dough is formed. Lay out on lightly floured surface; knead until smooth and elastic (about 15 minutes). Let rest, covered with cloth, about 30 minutes. Roll out dough about 1/16" thick (or less) and cut into 6" lengths about 1/4" to 1/16" wide.

Bob West

FRENCH ONION SOUP

1 T. unsalted butter
1 1/2 tsp. olive oil
1/2 lb. onions, thinly sliced
1/4 lb. leeks (white part only), thinly sliced
1 garlic clove, finely chopped
1/4 tsp. sugar
1 1/2 T. flour
4 cups heated beef broth or canned unsalted beef broth
1/4 cup dry vermouth
Dash of hot pepper sauce
Freshly ground pepper and salt
Toasted French bread slices
Thinly sliced Gruyère cheese

Serves 4.

Melt butter with oil in heavy large pot over low heat. Add onions, leeks and garlic and cook until onions soften, stirring occasionally, about 15 minutes. Increase heat to medium-low. Add sugar and cook until onions are deep golden brown, stirring frequently, about 30 minutes. Add flour and stir 3 minutes. Add stock, vermouth, hot pepper sauce and pepper. Simmer 40 minutes. Season with salt. (Can be prepared one day ahead. Cool, refrigerate. Reheat before continuing.)

Preheat broiler. Divide soup between soup crocks. Top each with toasted bread and several cheese slices. Broil until cheese melts and top is golden brown.

Becky Foley

Riding out the winter storms on a houseboat can be pretty scary. We bounce around a lot and, for those of us without insulated walls, the wind sometimes blows the curtains straight out into the room.

Houseboat Old-timer

*H*ouseboaters use a variety of means to keep their homes afloat. For a while, the most popular was big styrofoam blocks. On my dock, Ed and Karen learned one winter that it is possible to float too high in the water. They had a home built on a long skinny barge and had just poured a lot of time and effort into remodeling. Like most houseboats after a remodel, however, it was riding pretty low in the water. So, they contracted to have some styrofoam blocks set under the hull to raise it up a bit. Everything seemed fine until it snowed. No one was home that night, but next door, Gerta was hunkered down under the blankets trying to stay warm. About midnight she began to hear sounds like "ffwwtt-whoosh!" and tinkling like glass breaking. Peering through her window, she saw the new styrofoam blocks popping out from under her neighbors' house. The combination of the snow on

CURRIED CHICKEN-RICE SOUP

1 cup long grain brown rice
1/2 cup finely diced carrots
1/2 cup finely diced celery (cabbage or broccoli works too)
1 cup cooked chicken, diced
1 can cream of mushroom soup
3 1/2 cups water or chicken stock
1 tsp. salt
1/8 tsp. basil
1/4 tsp. curry (or to taste)
1/8 tsp. celery seeds
1/8 tsp. dill
1 T. finely diced pimiento

Serves 4.

Bring water to rolling boil, add salt and rice. Cook covered for 10 minutes. Add carrot, celery, curry and basil. Continue cooking on low heat, covered, until rice is soft. Add remaining ingredients and more water if necessary. Simmer 15 to 20 minutes. Serve with a dash of curry and basil.

T. G. Susor

COLD HERBED SWEET PEA-CUCUMBER SOUP

2 cups frozen peas
3-4 large cucumbers
1 T. vegetable oil
1/4 cup minced green onion
1 1/3 cups chicken broth
2 T. snipped fresh dill
1 tsp. salt
1/2 tsp. pepper
1 cup plain yogurt
Dill sprig or snipped dill for garnish

Serves 6-8.

Peel cucumbers, cut in half lengthwise and scoop out and discard seeds. Chop cucumber. Combine 1 cup peas, cucumber and remaining ingredients and puree in food processor. Add remaining peas to mixture and fold in. Chill. Dart each serving with 1 tablespoon of yogurt and garnish with dill sprig or snipped dill.

Bob Williams

top and the styrofoam underneath had made the barge top-heavy enough to begin to list. With each "ffwwtt-whoosh," Ed and Karen's house leaned more and more on its side. Gerta set about alerting the dock and calling for help. We woke up fast in the freezing air as we set up a chain gang to hand the valuables and furniture inside the house up to the dock. Finally, the police boat with the high-capacity pump arrived and the barge stopped sinking. By this time, almost everybody on the dock was awake. We distributed Ed and Karen's possessions to other houses for safe keeping. After everything was stashed away and the police boat's pump had stabilized the barge in the water, we all gathered in Gerta's kitchen for warm drinks and commentary on the night's events. It was nice to know you had neighbors who would turn out to help you in the middle of a snowy night.

Bill Keasler

SCOTCH BROTH

1 1/2 - 2 lbs. lamb blade steaks or other lean stew meat,
    preferably with bones
2 T. light olive oil
1/2 cup roughly chopped carrot
1/2 cup roughly chopped onion
1/2 cup roughly chopped celery
2 large cloves garlic, minced
1 T. sugar
1/4 cup fresh chopped parsley
6 cups water
1 bay leaf
1/2 tsp. thyme
3/4 tsp. salt
8-10 whole peppercorns
2 large carrots, diced
1 small white turnip, julienned
1/2 cup pearl barley
Parsley and lemon zest for garnish
Salt and pepper to taste

A memorable meal need be no more than a hearty homemade soup, crusty bread and a salad. This soup lends itself to ahead-of-time cooking and will refrigerate well for 3-4 days. Thin with canned chicken broth if necessary.

Serves 4-6.

Trim meat of fat and dredge lightly in seasoned flour. Heat oil in heavy pan, add meat and bones and brown well. Remove to soup kettle. Sauté the roughly cut carrots, onion and celery and garlic in the meat drippings for 1-2 minutes. Sprinkle sugar over vegetables and continue to cook, turning constantly. Vegetables should caramelize slightly but not burn. Add vegetables to meat and bones. Stir about a cup of water into the sauté pan, scrape up drippings and pour over meat and vegetables. Add remaining water, parsley, bay leaf, thyme, salt and peppercorns. Cover and bring to a boil. Reduce heat and simmer slowly for 2 hours.

Strain stock and degrease. Remove meat from the bones in bite-sized pieces. Combine strained stock and meat, add pearl barley and cook 30 minutes. Add diced carrots and turnip and cook an additional 20 minutes. Taste carefully for seasonings. Serve garnished with fresh parsley and a pinch of freshly grated lemon zest.

Gwen Bassetti

ALCHEMIST'S MUSHROOM SOUP

2 to 3 small boxes fresh mushrooms or 3 cans B&B
    buttered mushrooms
1 pkg. Lipton's cream of mushroom soup mix (or 2 pkgs.
    cup-of-soup mix)
1 can chicken broth (10 oz. or so)
1 13 oz. can evaporated milk

Serves 4-6.

If mushrooms are fresh, clean and put in double boiler along with a little butter and onion salt. Cook on medium heat for approximately 1 hour. Put mushrooms (either fresh or directly from cans) along with juice in blender and chop into small bits.

Combine chicken broth with cream of mushroom soup mix in double boiler and heat slowly. Add evaporated milk and mushrooms. Heat thoroughly.

Anne Helmholz

*T*his recipe is my father's creation which matches the taste and consistency of an elegant soup his grandmother used to make, but is much simpler. As he set about duplicating her recipe, his comment to me was, "it's simply a matter of chemistry, Anne." I say if chemistry can help us eat this well, then I'm all for it!

Seattle, Washington

CHOPPY CARROT SOUP

2 slices bacon, diced
1/4 cup chopped onion
1 clove garlic, crushed
2 cans chicken broth
2 cups chopped carrots
1 cup diced potatoes
1 medium tomato, chopped
1 tsp. salt
Dash pepper

Garnish:
sour cream
Parsley
Shredded carrots

The first winter on my houseboat, the roof in the bathroom leaked so badly that I finally took a big sheet of black plastic and nailed it to all four corners of the room and funneled the drips down through a hole in the floor into the lake.

Houseboat Old-timer

Serves 4.

Sauté bacon, onion, and garlic until bacon is crisp. Stir in remaining ingredients, heat to boiling point. Reduce heat and simmer until vegetables are tender, 15 to 20 minutes. Pour into blender, blend at high speed until smooth. For thinner consistency, use more chicken broth.

Serve with sour cream, parsley, and shredded carrots.

Nancy Johnson

APPLE & CHEDDAR BISQUE

1 T. olive oil
1 small onion, peeled and finely chopped
1 celery stalk, finely diced
1 small carrot, peeled and finely diced
1 clove garlic, minced
2 medium white potatoes, peeled and cut into 1/2" cubes
2 medium Granny Smith apples, peeled and cut into 1/2" cubes
3 cups water
1/2 cup dry white wine
1/2 tsp. dried thyme, divided
3/4 tsp. salt
1/8 tsp. freshly ground black pepper
1/8 tsp. cayenne pepper
1 1/2 cups (about 4 oz.) low-fat cheddar cheese, coarsely
   shredded
1/2 cup half & half
2 tsp. lemon juice

Serves 4.

In a large sauce pan or Dutch oven, heat the olive oil over medium heat.
Add the onion and sauté until softened, about 5 minutes. Add the
celery, carrot and garlic and sauté 2 minutes.

Stir in the potatoes, apples, water, wine, 1/4 tsp. thyme, salt, pepper and
cayenne. Bring to a boil. Reduce heat and simmer for 30 minutes, until
the vegetables are very soft.

Purée the soup in a food processor, adding the remaining 1/4 tsp.
thyme, cheese and half & half. Process until smooth. Strain through a
sieve. Pour back into a clean saucepan and place on medium-low just
to heat through. Stir in the lemon juice and serve.

June Fauchald

During one winter storm a houseboat on our dock tipped over from the weight of the snow on the roof. No crane company would touch it because of the liability, so George Johnston, our "flotation man", came to the rescue and began stuffing styrofoam logs under the house, one after the other. Most of the dock residents were outside watching him, and, at the same time, watching a football game on a portable TV on the dock. We were glued to the TV for a crucial touchdown, and when we turned back to check George's progress, the houseboat had popped up and was back in its upright position!

Houseboat Old-timer

LENTIL AND SAUSAGE SOUP

1 pkg. (1 lb.) lentils
4 1/2 cups boiling water
2 tsp. salt
2 cloves garlic, minced
1 lb. Italian sausages
1 large onion, chopped
1 large carrot, chopped
8 oz. tomato sauce
3 T. vinegar

Serves 4-6.

In large (4 quart) baking dish, combine lentils with boiling water, salt and garlic. Cover and put in 350 F. oven. Remove casings from sausages and cut into 1" chunks. Brown, drain (save 2 T. drippings) and set aside. To 2 T. drippings add onion and carrots to sauté. Add meat, onions and carrots to lentils. Bake for 45 minutes covered. Add tomato sauce and vinegar and bake uncovered another 20 minutes.

Bruce Knott

SAILOR'S SOUR CHERRY SAUCE

1 1/2 cups sour cherries
1/2 cup Port
1/4 cup red currant jelly
1 T. Dijon mustard
1/3 cup lemon juice
1/4 cup orange juice
1 tsp. grated orange rind

Makes 2 cups.

In a saucepan simmer sour cherries in Port for 10 minutes. Let the mixture cool completely. In a small saucepan set over hot water soften (but do not melt) red currant jelly. Transfer the jelly to a small bowl and combine it with Dijon mustard, lemon juice, orange juice, and grated orange rind. Stir in the cherry mixture.

Mary Gey

*S*erve this special sauce with "Roast Pork" and "Roaring Rice Salad" (see recipes).

I have been making hot sauce for years and friends always consume it with tears in their eyes and a drink close by, knowing they'll pay the consequences the next day. They also hang around my kitchen when I make a batch (gallons) and everyone always wants a jar of their own. My dad once put some in a catsup bottle and sealed it with a cork. Later he claimed the hot sauce "ate" the cork.

[Editor's Note: A tendency toward inflammable sauces must run in the family. Jann's father is Art Hemenway, who is famous for his "Fatal Feta" and "Scurvy Preventer" — as well as his tango!]

EXTERMINATOR RED HOT SAUCE

6 or so dried cayenne or other red hot peppers
1 12-oz. to 15-oz. can tomatoes
1 small (8-oz.) can tomato sauce
4 canned or fresh jalapeno peppers
1 medium sized dry onion
2 cloves garlic
1 T. each cumin and oregano
1/3 to 1/2 cup vinegar
Salt and pepper to taste

Makes about 1 quart.

Remove stems from hot peppers. Put all ingredients in blender and blend on medium speed until everything is finely minced, but not lique-fied, or too foamy. Cook about 30 to 40 minutes over medium heat. Taste. If too hot, add more tomatoes; if too mild, add peppers. Put in jars and keep in ice box. Lasts indefinitely. (Be careful handling chiles as the oil in them will burn your fingers, even if you use soap and water. Wear rubber gloves, don't rub eyes, etc.)

Jann McFarland

MARIE'S BARBECUE SAUCE

1/2 tsp. cayenne pepper
1/2 tsp. black pepper
2 T. vinegar
2 T. A-1 sauce
1 tsp. chili powder
1 tsp. paprika
3/4 cup catsup
3/4 cup water

Makes about 1 1/2 cups.

Mix all ingredients, pour over spareribs and bake until meat is tender.

Marie Johnston

Marie's husband, Leonard, has lived in houseboats on Lake Union for more than 40 years, and Marie joined him more than 25 years ago. They've lived on both sides of the lake at one time or another and have literally watched generations come and go. They have seen the docks change from rows of sprung roof shacks to modern two-story "mansions". The Johnstons have lived at their current end-tie location on the west side of the lake since about 1967. You can't miss their bright turquoise home or them sitting on their spacious deck on a summer evening watching the Duck Dodge sailboat race and enjoying a cool one with their neighbors. And, if you ever have a question about Lake Union history, just stop by and ask — they remember it all!

Low Fat Sauce Medley

Mustard Tarragon Sauce (for fish, chicken or veggies)

2 tsp. tarragon vinegar *
2 tsp. dry mustard (or 4 tsp. Dijon)
Salt & pepper to taste
2 T. flour (or corn starch or potato starch)
1 cup skim milk

Makes about 1 cup.

Mix the flour with a little of the milk to make a thin paste. Heat the rest of the milk on very low heat until warm. Gradually mix warm milk with the paste to avoid lumps. Put back on the low heat, whisk in salt and pepper and keep whisking until thick. Then whisk in the mustard and vinegar at the last second.

*Grow some tarragon in a pot on your deck. Put some sprigs in a bottle and add plain white or white wine vinegar. Let sit for a week before using.

Prune Sauce (for shrimp, fish, chicken, pork & rice)

3/4 cup Madeira wine
1/2 cup beef broth (canned is fine)
1 T. red wine vinegar
3 whole cloves
12 or so pitted prunes
2 T. cornstarch

Makes about 2 cups.

Mix cornstarch with a little of the stock to make a thin paste. Heat everything but the cornstarch and the prunes until just boiling. Add cornstarch and cook, stirring, until thickened. Add prunes and heat through.

If you are trying to trim off those love handles and reduce the need for more flotation, here's a collection of tasty no-fat sauces to perk up that skinned chicken, white fish, trimmed pork, pasta and veggies.

Spicy Soy & Chili Sauce (for shrimp, white fish, chicken or sliced pork)

1/8-1/4 tsp. chili paste with garlic (Asian section of grocery)
1/4 cup soy sauce
1/2 cup chicken stock (go ahead -- buy canned)
2 T. red wine vinegar
2 tsp. cornstarch dissolved in a couple teaspoons water

Makes 3/4 cup.

Heat everything except the cornstarch in a sauce pan, whisking, until boiling. Add cornstarch and keep cooking and whisking until sauce thickens.

Quickie Rice Vinegar Sauce (for steamed veggies, pasta or fish)

1/2 cup rice vinegar (seasoned, unseasoned, light or dark)
1 T. sugar
1/2 tsp. soy sauce
3 or 4 drops sesame oil (optional)

Heat vinegar, sugar and soy sauce until sugar dissolves. Add the sesame oil. We like this on broccoli the best!

Beth Means

One winter we kept seeing peeled logs floating by our houseboat. Always in the market for free firewood, we took the logs into the house and burned them. We finally found out that beavers, who had built a house at the shore end of our dock, were stealing the wood from our neighbor's deck, eating the bark, and discarding the logs into the lake.

ITALIAN BBQ SAUCE

1 8 oz. can tomato sauce
3 T. olive oil
3 T. red wine vinegar or red wine
1 tsp. dried mixed Italian herbs
1/2 tsp. fresh rosemary, minced
2 T. fresh basil leaves, chopped
3 cloves garlic, minced
1 T. red pepper flakes (or to taste)
Salt and pepper to taste

Makes about 1 1/4 cups.

Mix all ingredients with a whisk until blended. Brush on chicken during the last few minutes on the grill. Great on thick slices of eggplant or Japanese eggplants sliced in half lengthwise and laid on grill. Also good on zucchini, bell peppers and onions. Do not overcook vegetables.

Jann McFarland

FIRST PRIZE BBQ SAUCE

1/2 cup olive oil
3 T. red wine vinegar
2 T. red pepper flakes (or to taste)
4 garlic cloves, grated
1 tsp. dried thyme
Salt and fresh ground black pepper to taste

Makes 3/4 cup.

Whisk ingredients together. Grill food over slow fire, then paint with sauce. Turn food and paint with sauce. Turn a second time for each side. Remove from grill to serving platter and brush once more.

Sid and Jann McFarland

This sauce is great on almost anything grilled. Try halved zucchini, broccoli, halved new potatoes, corn on the cob, bell pepper strips, halved onions (especially sweets), or combine them all on kabobs. It's also good on chicken, ribs and beef strips. This recipe won the potluck contest at a dock party one summer. It was cold and drizzly and we cooked red potatoes on the grill. I suspect we won because people were putting the potatoes in their pockets to keep warm rather than eating them!

CREAMY CASHEW CHUTNEY

1 cup raw cashews
1/4 tsp. lemon juice
1 tsp. salt
1/2" piece fresh ginger root, peeled and sliced
1 or 2 hot green chiles, seeded and chopped
Up to 1/3 cup water
2 T. fresh coriander, chopped

Yields 1 1/4 cups.

Combine cashews, lemon juice, salt, ginger, chiles and 1/4 cup water in a blender and process. Add more water if necessary to make a loose purée. Place in a bowl and add fresh coriander. This sauce will thicken over time; add water to thin to desired consistency. Can be stored, covered, in refrigerator for up to 3 days.

Mike Dash

This is about as perfect a recipe as I've ever seen — easy to make, versatile and delicious. Use sauce to accompany Indian dishes, raw vegetables or thin it to make a salad dressing.

DATE AND RAISIN CHUTNEY

1/2 tsp. fennel seeds
1 tsp. cumin seeds
1/2 T. coriander seeds
1 cup chopped, pitted dates
1/3 cup raisins (preferably muscat)
1/4 cup fresh lime juice
2 T. fresh orange juice
1/2" piece fresh ginger root, peeled and sliced
2 or 3 hot jalapeno chiles, seeded and chopped
1/4 tsp. salt
1/8 tsp. freshly ground nutmeg
2 T. fresh coriander, chopped

Yields 1 1/2 cups.

Slowly dry roast spice seeds in heavy pan over low heat. When darkened a few shades, remove from heat and cool. Combine the dates, raisins and citrus juices in a small bowl and let sit for 2 hours. In a blender or food processor, mince together ginger and chiles. Add soaked fruit and seeds and process until coarsely ground. Transfer to a bowl and stir in salt, nutmeg and fresh coriander. Cover and refrigerate. Will keep 5 to 6 days.

Mike Dash

Most people live in their floating homes. Patricia Bowman, a concert pianist, used hers as a concert hall. She is warmly remembered by her dockmates for giving recitals on either of her 2 baby grand pianos, in her Portage Bay houseboat.

Houseboat Harry

Seattle, Washington

APPLE MINT JELLY

4-5 lbs. green apples
3 cups water
1 T. lemon juice, strained
7 1/2 cups sugar
1 cup chopped fresh mint
1 pouch Certo fruit pectin
Green food coloring

Makes 4 pints.

A classic with lamb . . . and a wonderful gift combo with Red Pepper Jelly (see recipe)!

Remove stems and blossoms from apples. Cut in small pieces (do not peel or core). Place in large saucepan. Add water and bring to a boil. Cover and simmer 10 minutes. Stir to crush apples. Cover and cook 5-10 minutes longer until apples are completely cooked and make sauce when stirred. Place 3 layers of cheese cloth or a jelly bag on a large bowl and pour cooked apples into cheesecloth. Tie ends of cheese cloth and hang over bowl until dripping stops. Press bag lightly. (Note: the less you squeeze the bag the clearer your jelly will be.)

Measure lemon juice and apple juice to make 5 cups (add a small amount of water if necessary) into a 6-8 quart saucepan. Stir in sugar and mint and mix well. Bring to a full, rolling boil over high heat, stirring constantly. Boil 2 minutes. Add Certo and continue boiling for 2 more minutes. Remove from heat and skim off any foam. Add a few drops of green food coloring if necessary. Fill hot jars and seal immediately. Jelly will keep several months in the refrigerator.

Gwen Bassetti

My Mother's Red Pepper Jelly

3 large red bell peppers, puréed (about 1 1/2 cups)
3 small hot red peppers, puréed (about 1/2 cup)
3/4 cup white vinegar
3 1/2 cups sugar
1 3 oz. pkg. Certo pectin or equivalent dry pectin

Makes 2 1/2 pints

Seed peppers thoroughly and remove excess pulp. Cut in rough chunks and purée in a food processor or blender. Mix peppers with vinegar in a 4-5 quart pan. Add pectin and bring to a boil. Add sugar and boil hard, stirring constantly for 10 minutes, or until a spoonful jells when cooled on a plate. Pour into hot jars and seal. Will keep several months in the refrigerator.

Gwen Bassetti

Wonderful with chicken or sausages, and a winner as a quick hors d'oeuvre. Top any good cracker with cream cheese and dot with a half teaspoon of red pepper jelly. Take my word and try it!

CATTAILS, WILD IRIS AND LILY PADS

Salads

*I*n our sunny deck planters we grow many flowers, herbs and vegetables, including jalapeno, cayenne and yellow and red bell peppers, Japanese eggplant, zucchini, summer squash, cucumbers, tomatoes, green onions, lettuce, chard, green beans, sugar peas, blueberries, strawberries, parsley, rosemary, basil, tarragon, chives, thyme, mint, oregano, sage, lavender and even corn and brussel sprouts. A neighbor, originally from Texas, grows pinto beans and grapes in his planters. Another neighbor has a row of big, fat sunflowers and two apple trees. We also tried water chestnuts on a little float one year.

Jann McFarland

INDONESIAN RICE SALAD

2 cups basmati rice
2 green peppers, seeded and chopped
3/4 cup scallions, chopped
1 cup raw cashews
1 7 oz. can sliced water chestnuts
Juice of 1 lemon
1/2 cup orange juice
1/2 cup safflower oil
1/4 cup soy sauce

Serves 8

Steam rice for 20 minutes. Combine rice with remaining ingredients and let sit 2 or more hours.

Jaqueline Hightower

SPINACH AND KIWI SALAD

3 cups spinach
1 cup mustard greens or any tart crisp green
2 cups red-leaf lettuce
1 large ripe kiwi
1 small red onion
2 T. oil
2 T. honey (approx.)
Juice of 1 lemon
1 clove garlic, slivered
Salt and freshly ground white pepper

Serves 4-6.

Remove stems from spinach and greens and discard. Wash spinach, greens and lettuce and dry in salad spinner. Tear into bite-sized pieces. Place greens in salad bowl, cover with plastic wrap and refrigerate. Peel and slice kiwi. Peel onion and cut into thin slices. Place kiwi and onion slices on small plate, cover with plastic wrap and refrigerate. In small bowl, combine remaining ingredients and whisk until ready to serve salad. Remove garlic just before tossing greens with dressing. Toss greens with dressing, divide among individual salad bowls and garnish with kiwi and red onion.

Becky Foley

This salad is good with grilled fish.

TORTELLINI SALAD

1/2 lb. cheese or meat filled tortellini, fresh or frozen
2 cups cauliflower flowerets
2 cups broccoli flowerets
4 green onions, chopped
1/2 cup black olives, pitted and sliced
1/4 lb. fresh mushrooms, sliced
1 egg yolk
1 T. Dijon mustard
1 small clove garlic, finely minced
2 T. wine vinegar
2 T. dry vermouth
1 tsp. Worcestershire sauce
1/2 cup vegetable or olive oil
Salt and freshly ground pepper
1/3 cup heavy cream
Boston lettuce leaves for garnish
1 pint cherry tomatoes for garnish

Serves 6.

Bring water to boil in large pot for pasta and in large saucepan for
vegetables. Cook tortellini in boiling water until just done. Fresh
tortellini will take about 5 minutes, frozen about 6 — watch carefully
and do not overcook. Stir occasionally. When done, drain tortellini
well in colander and then transfer to large bowl.

Cook cauliflower 3 minutes in saucepan of boiling water; add broccoli
and cook 2 minutes more. Drain well, and run under cold water to stop
cooking.

Combine egg yolk, mustard and garlic in small bowl and beat with
whisk. Beat in vinegar, vermouth and Worcestershire sauce. Slowly
add oil, whisking vigorously until creamy. Add salt and pepper to taste.

Gently fold cooked and raw vegetables into pasta (except cherry
tomatoes), together with enough dressing to moisten well. Use rubber
spatula in order not to break up tortellini or vegetables. Let stand at
room temperature until ready to serve.

Just before serving, add cream and toss again. Serve on lettuce-lined
platter with border of cherry tomatoes.

Becky Foley

4th of July Spaghetti Salad

2 T. oil in boiling water
1 tsp. salt
1 small pkg. spaghetti
1 small bottle Italian dressing
1 can chopped olives
1/2 cup onions, chopped fine
1 large tomato, diced
1 stalk celery, chopped
1/2 small jar pimientos
Broccoli, chopped (optional)
Green and/or red peppers, chopped (optional)

Serves 2-4.

Bring water to boil with oil and salt, add spaghetti and cook for 10 minutes. Drain into a colander and rinse. Mix remaining ingredients and toss with spaghetti. Sprinkle with paprika and parsley.

Keith Lockwood and Anthony Edwards

Canoeing through the throngs on Lake Union is one of my favorite 4th of July activities. One year we saw five young "hard bodies" leap off a 2nd story roof to the accompaniment of a rock band on a nearby roof deck. When these guys arose from the depths, my friend called to them that they looked great but she didn't have her camera ready. "Could you guys go up and jump off again, only this time do it together!" The surf was aboil as they swam back to the house, flew up to the roof, flexed, posed, then leapt off the roof in unison. They were gorgeous! When they again rose from the deep, she said, "That was great, but I didn't have any film in my camera — can you do it again, only this time . . . ." The next five cannonballs swamped the canoe, but we escaped . . . and we were kidding about the film and have the photos to prove it.

Anonymous Admirer

Our softball team, the
"Environmental Wastrels", only
won one game (the other team
forfeited). But we got better, to the
point where we no longer lost by 30
points! And we had a lot of fun.
At the end of the season we passed
out "awards" on my houseboat roof
during the Duck Dodge sailboat
race. CJ's contribution to the
potluck was always appreciated.

Sheri Lockwood

CJ'S CABBAGE SALAD

1 pkg. chicken flavored Top Ramen
2 T. sesame seeds
1/2 cup slivered almonds
1/2 large head cabbage, shredded
4 green onions, chopped
1/2 cup vegetable oil
2 T. sugar
3 T. vinegar
1 tsp. salt
1/2 tsp. pepper

Serves 4.

Toast almonds and sesame seeds in shallow pan at 350 F. for 5 to 10 minutes. Combine Top Ramen flavor packet, sugar, salt, and pepper. Add vinegar and stir, then add the oil. Combine all parts and toss well.

C.J. Eriksen

QUICK CAESAR SALAD

1 crushed garlic bud
1/2 tsp. salt
1/4 tsp. pepper
1/2 tsp. dry mustard
1 T. lemon juice
1/4 cup oil
2-3 T. grated parmesan cheese
Romaine lettuce leaves, torn
Tomato wedges

Serves 2.

Use a wooden salad bowl. Mix first seven ingredients in bottom of
bowl. Add lettuce to bowl. Do not toss. Cover and let stand several
hours. Add tomato wedges and toss. Serve immediately.

Theresa Harvey

Houseboat docks have many wild inhabitants (in addition to the humans, that is). Ducks, geese and raccoons are on every dock. It's generally pleasant to have these creatures around, but they do cause the occasional grievance by nesting in or eating our garden plants or swiping the cat's food. Coots, grebes, scaups, herons and other waterfowl come and go with the seasons. Less frequently we spot an otter or beaver. Because Lake Union is fresh water, there is no resident population of seals or sea lions—although there are rare reports of such animals that apparently slip through the locks.
Ann Bassetti

Many homeowners have experienced a horrendous smell announcing that some poor animal met its end beneath their house. Houseboaters can have the same problem, but for us it's often a migrating salmon that lost its way! I had one a few years ago that was so far underneath my house and smelled so disgusting, that I hired a diver to retrieve it!

Bonnie Morrison

ROARING RICE SALAD

3 cups steamed rice
1/2 cup radishes, thinly sliced
1/2 cup scallions, thinly sliced
1 green pepper, minced
2 T. minced gherkin pickle
1 T. minced parsley
1 T. snipped dill
1 T. snipped chives
Salt and pepper to taste

Dressing:
1 tsp. mustard
1 cup mayonnaise

Let rice cool to room temperature. Toss the rice with 3/4 cup dressing. Add remaining ingredients and mix well. Serve with "Roast Pork" (see recipe).

Mary Gey

DUTCH'S HAND-CARVED SHRIMP SALAD

1 small redwood log hollowed out to make a bowl
1 lb. fresh shrimp
Lettuce leaves
2 green peppers, chopped
1 green onion, chopped
2-3 Italian tomatoes, chopped
1/2 small pimiento
Ripe olives
1 quartered hard boiled egg
Italian dressing

Serves 2.

Catch a log drifting by and spend 3 years carving a glorious bowl. Then spend 5 minutes mixing the above ingredients to go in it. Garnish with wood chips and sawdust (optional).

Friends of Dutch Schultz

Dutch Schultz is a marvelous Northwest wood sculptor and has been an institution on the house-boats for more than 20 years. He doesn't cook much, so we put one in for him on the grounds that it might encourage him to try it.

Duck Dodge — Lake Union's No Class Race With Class — God's Chosen Race! Every Tuesday night of the summer, since 1974, every imaginable kind of sail-powered vessel has gathered on the lake for the 7:00 p.m. start of the race. In August of 1991, 110 boats were counted participating! The first Duck Dodge was raced between a couple of guys, one of whom was a houseboater, just trying to see whose boat was the fastest. They had so much fun they made up some posters and tacked them up around the lake announcing the "Lake Union Beer Can Regatta or Tenas Chuck Duck Dodge". The only rule was the "Scared Duck Rule". "Any yacht coming in contact with or substantially frightening any duck shall complete a 720 degree turn and apologize to the duck before continuing." Over the years other rules have been added — such as penalties for

(cont'd. next page)

CRAB SALAD

1 box prepared Uncle Ben's Long Grain and Wild Rice
1 package frozen black eyed peas, thawed
1 package frozen green peas, thawed
1 green bell pepper, chopped
1 red bell pepper, chopped
1-2 lbs. minced crab meat (3-4 cans)
3-4 finely chopped celery stalks, including leaves
1/4 cup chopped parsley
Juice of 2 lemons

Serves 4-6.

Mix all ingredients and chill. Serve as a side dish or on lettuce. May also be served with buttermilk dressing.

Bob Williams

insufficient bribery of the race committee — though none very serious. Prizes have ranged from a rubber duck which the winner (or was it loser?) had to tow around until the next race and bottles of Pusser's Rum, to the coveted gold, silver and bronze ducky stickers, the status symbols of yacht racing. This race is so famous that in 1987, the America's Cup 12 Meter, "Stars and Stripes", came to Seattle and raced 3 Duck Dodges to tune up for the cup race! And theme nights give racers the chance to shed normal yachting attire for grass skirts (Hawaiian Night), wigs and coconuts (Ladies Night, where all crew must be or look like ladies), PJ's (Pajama Night) or top hats (Hat Night). The season ends the Tuesday after Labor Day with Committee Boat Appreciation Night, where the prudent skipper can set himself up for the next year of Duck Dodging by generous bribery of the liquid variety!

A Deck Chair Dodger

NO PEEKEE POKER SALAD

12 oz. crab or shrimp
1 pkg. (10 oz.) frozen peas, thawed and drained
1 T. lemon juice
1 T. soy sauce
1 can (3 oz.) chow mein noodles
1/2 cup toasted almonds
1/2 cup chopped celery
1/2 cup sliced water chestnuts
5 green onions, chopped
3/4 cup mayonnaise
1/2 tsp. curry
1/2 tsp. garlic

Serves 6.

Dry crab or shrimp well. Mix all ingredients except noodles, almonds and crab or shrimp. Add these at the last minute (so it won't get soggy).

Leslie Rubicam

BREAD SALAD WITH ROASTED FARM VEGETABLES

Serve this flavorful salad as an appetizer or as a complement to grilled meats. Good chilled or at room temperature, this salad makes a perfect addition to the picnic basket. Gwen's Grand Central Bakery in Pioneer Square is largely responsible for the renaissance of rustic breads in Seattle. Luckily for us houseboaters, GCB breads are available at many of our neighborhood markets.

4 or 5 slices thick-sliced rustic bread, cubed (3-4 cups)
2 T. chopped parsley
1 T. chopped chives
1 tsp. dried tarragon leaves
2 large cloves garlic, minced
3/4 cup grated Parmesan cheese
1 pint cherry tomatoes
1 small zucchini, sliced
1 small yellow summer squash, sliced
1 medium Japanese eggplant, diced (about 1 cup)
2-3 T. olive oil
Salt and pepper to taste
1 small red onion, very thinly sliced
2 T. capers

Dressing:
2/3 cup olive oil
2 T. red wine vinegar

Serves 6-8.

Toss cubed bread with parsley, chives, tarragon, garlic and Parmesan cheese. Spread in a shallow pan and toast in a 325 F. oven for 20-30 minutes or until crisp and golden brown. Remove and cool.

Toss cherry tomatoes, squash and eggplant with oil and salt and pepper, spread on the shallow roasting pan. Turn the heat to 375 F. and roast 20-30 minutes. Cool.

Combine toasted bread, cooled vegetables, red onion and capers. Blend olive oil and vinegar and drizzle over salad. Serve on bed of fresh arugula.

Gwen Bassetti

DIJONAISE POTATO SALAD

1 cup Best Foods mayonnaise
1/4 cup Best Foods Dijonaise creamy mustard blend
2 T. vinegar
2 T. chopped fresh dill or parsley
1/2 tsp. salt
1/4 tsp. pepper
2 lbs. small red or all purpose potatoes, cooked and cubed
1 cup sliced celery
1/2 cup sliced green onions

Makes 6 cups.

In a large bowl combine first 6 ingredients. Stir in potatoes, celery and onions. Cover and chill.

Carolyn Bland

OKLAHOMA COLE SLAW

*M*y mother got this recipe from a
friend, who got it from her mother,
who got it from a friend, who used
to serve it at church suppers in
Oklahoma. I make it the day before
the 2025 Luau. Then I don't have
to worry about cooking and can
drink lots of punch.

1 medium head cabbage, shredded
1 medium onion, thinly sliced
1/2 cup sugar

Dressing:
1/2 cup vinegar
2/3 cup salad oil
1 T. celery seed
2 T. sugar
1 T. salt
Pepper to taste

Serves 6-8.

Layer cabbage and onion in a bowl. Sprinkle with sugar. Mix all dressing ingredients in saucepan and bring to a boil. While hot, pour over cabbage mixture. Do not stir. Cover and let stand overnight. It will keep in the refrigerator for several days.

Anne LeVasseur

LOG FOUNDATION
CABBAGE SALAD

1/2 head red cabbage
1/2 head green cabbage
1 bunch green onions, chopped
1 pkg. frozen peas, thawed and drained
1 cup shredded carrots
1 cup chopped water chestnuts
1/2 cup slivered almonds, toasted
1/2 cup sesame seeds, toasted
1 pkg. chicken flavored Top Ramen noodles, uncooked
    and crumbled

Dressing:
1/2 cup salad oil
1 T. sesame oil
3 T. rice vinegar
Seasoning packet from Top Ramen

Serves 6.

Mix all ingredients. Before serving, mix dressing and toss on salad.

Kris Eaton

The Log Foundation is a cooperatively owned moorage consisting of 52 houseboats on 3 docks, located in the southeastern part of Lake Union. After participating in the battles to protect our houseboats over the years, it was a great relief to finally buy our moorage.

CHILLED ORIENTAL NOODLE SALAD

1 3 oz. pkg. chicken-flavored Japanese noodles
3 T. vegetable oil
1 tsp. sesame oil
Dash chili oil
2 T. rice wine vinegar
1 tsp. sugar
Salt and pepper to taste
1/4 cup very thin zucchini slices
1/4 cup shredded carrots
1 T. chopped green onion
1 clove garlic, minced
1/4 lb. cooked shrimp
2 T. toasted slivered almonds

2 servings, easily doubled.

Bring 2 cups of water to boil. Break noodles in several places before opening package. Remove seasoning packet and set aside. Cook noodles over medium heat for 3 minutes, stirring occasionally. Reserve 1 tsp. of seasoning mix for dressing. Remove noodles from heat and stir in remainder of seasoning packet. Drain, then chill.

Combine reserved seasoning mix, vegetable, sesame and chili oils, rice wine vinegar and sugar and season to taste with salt and pepper. Mix well. Add dressing, zucchini, carrot, green onion, garlic and shrimp to noodles. Refrigerate.

Sprinkle almonds over salad just before serving.

Karen Hayes

As he sat fishing on his Portage Bay dock, Jim Gray was adopted by Leon, a cat. They became such good friends that Jim fished for Leon's dinner every night for years thereafter.

Colleen Hogan-Taylor

CHICKEN OR PRAWN CASHEW SALAD

1 cup cooked, shredded chicken breast or
    same amount of cooked, shelled, deveined small prawns
1/2 cup chopped celery
2 green onions, chopped, including tops
1/2 cup (or more) whole cashews

Dressing:
1/2 cup mayonnaise
1/2 lemon, juiced
2 T. curry powder (or to taste)
Dash cayenne
Salt and pepper to taste

Serves 2.

Combine chicken or shrimp, celery and green onions in bowl. Mix dressing ingredients. Add cashews to salad at last minute and pour on dressing and toss. Divide among 2 plates and serve on lettuce leaves. Recipe can easily be enlarged for more servings.

Jann McFarland

When we first got our kitten, Max, our older cat, Caruso, was really bent out of shape. One day Max was stalking Caruso, who was just sitting on the edge of the deck enjoying the sun. As Max pounced on Caruso, Caruso stepped aside and Max flew through the air like a flying squirrel and landed in the lake. Caruso was definitely smiling.

CHINESE PORK SALAD

1 lb. pork strips
1/2 cup Oriental stir fry sauce
3 green onions, sliced
1/2 red bell pepper, diced
2 10 oz. pkgs. frozen pea pods, thawed and drained
1 8 oz. can mandarin oranges, drained
1 3 oz. can chow mein noodles

Serves 4-6.

Marinate pork strips in stir fry sauce. In large skillet, stir fry pork over medium heat about 4-5 minutes. In large bowl toss pork with remaining ingredients. Serve with hot French bread.

Carolyn Bland

Chinese Chicken Salad

1 chicken breast, boned, skinned, cooked and shredded
4 T. toasted sesame seeds
4 T. slivered almonds
1 head cabbage, sliced
3 or 4 green onions, sliced
3 pkgs. ramen noodles, uncooked and crumbled

Dressing:
4 T. sugar
1 cup minus 2 T. vegetable oil
1 tsp. salt
1 tsp. MSG (optional)
1/2 tsp. pepper
6 T. rice vinegar
2-3 T. lemon juice
2 T. sesame oil

Serves 4-6 as main course.

Combine dressing ingredients in blender. Mix salad ingredients and toss with dressing.

Bruce Knott

When we lived in a houseboat at the north end of Lake Union in the late 60's, the old-timer next to us still abided by the old ways. Each morning he would dump his breakfast scraps out the kitchen window — straight into the lake. I could always tell what he'd eaten for breakfast as I'd watch the grapefruit peels, egg shells, banana peels, or whatever bobbing down the channel.

Marianne Kenady

An ornamental fig tree blew into the lake one afternoon. It was a big one in a pot and so a diver was called. He didn't find the fig tree, but he did find the neighbor's old dead potted Christmas tree from several years before which they had surreptitiously dropped overboard in the dead of night. It was covered with black smelly Lake Union sludge and was promptly put back on their deck to surprise them.

WHITE BEAN SALAD

1 lb. pkg. Great Northern beans
4 T. chopped fresh basil
1 T. chopped mint leaves
4 T. chopped parsley
1/2 green bell pepper, chopped
3-4 green onions, chopped (include tops)
Cherry tomatoes, halved (garnish)

Dressing
4 T. olive oil
4 T. white vinegar
1 T. Dijon mustard
Tabasco sauce to taste
Black pepper to taste

Serves 4-6.

Cover beans with water and bring to a boil. Then turn off burner and let beans soak 1 hour. Drain off water. Put in new water to cover beans and cook about 1/2 hour to 45 minutes. Do not overcook or beans will be mushy. Pour into a colander and run cold water over beans to stop cooking.

Whisk together the vinegar, oil, mustard, Tabasco and pepper until blended.

Combine beans with basil, mint, parsley, green pepper, and green onions. Toss with dressing. Let sit for several hours at room temperature before serving. Garnish with halved cherry tomatoes.

Jann McFarland

3-BEAN DELI SALAD

2 cans mixed yellow wax & green beans, drained
1 can garbanzo beans, drained
1 can red kidney beans, drained
1 small jar marinated artichoke hearts, halved, with liquid
1 cup large stuffed green olives, cut in half
1 green bell pepper, chopped
1/2 cup thinly sliced red onion rings

Dressing:
2/3 cup vinegar
1/2 cup sugar
1/2 cup salad oil
1 clove garlic, split
1 tsp. salt
1/2 tsp. Worcestershire sauce
1/8 tsp. pepper

Serves 6.

Mix salad ingredients in large bowl. Mix dressing ingredients in a jar
and shake well. Throw out the garlic clove. Pour dressing over bean
mixture and refrigerate for 2 or 3 hours. Serve on lettuce or by itself.

Sandi McQuirk

CAESAR SALAD

2 heads romaine lettuce
2 "coddled" eggs
1/2 cup Parmesan cheese

Dressing:
1 cup olive oil
Juice of 1 lemon
1/4 cup seasoned rice vinegar
1 garlic clove, pressed
1 T. sugar
Salt and pepper
1 T. anchovy paste

Croutons:
6-8 slices Grand Central Bakery "Como" bread, 3/4" thick,
    diced
1 clove garlic, minced
3 T. butter
4 T. olive oil

Serves 8-10.

To "coddle" eggs, drop in boiling water for 90 seconds. Run under cold water. To make dressing, combine ingredients in blender or food processor and blend for 30-40 seconds. To make croutons, melt butter in a large frying pan, add oil and garlic and toss in bread. Stir and cook over medium low heat until crisp and brown (about 15 minutes). To assemble salad, chop romaine and place in large salad bowl. Break coddled eggs over lettuce, add croutons, dressing and Parmesan. Toss well. Taste and season with salt and freshly ground black pepper.

Gwen Bassetti

*O*n a stifling summer night, we left our door open seeking to catch a breeze. We were stunned to awaken in the middle of the night with masked intruders in the bedroom -- raccoons trying to turn on the TV!

Tom Carlson & Janeel Eddie

MALLARD COVE
TORTELLINI SALAD

14 oz. tortellini, any kind
1/3 cup olive oil
1/4 cup garlic flavored red wine vinegar
2 T. Worcestershire sauce
3 T. Dijon mustard
1 1/2 tsp. pepper
1 large clove garlic, minced
2 T. sugar
2 tsp. salt
2 dashes Tabasco
1 cup sliced celery
1 cup chopped green onions
1 cup mushrooms, sliced thin
1 cup grated sharp cheddar cheese
1/3 cup chopped pimiento
2 T. chopped parsley

Serves 6.

Cook tortellini in large pot of boiling water. Drain and rinse in cold water and transfer to a medium size bowl. Toss with olive oil.

In another bowl, mix vinegar, Worcestershire, mustard, pepper, garlic, sugar, salt and Tabasco, blending well. Add celery, green onions, mushrooms, cheese and pimiento and mix well. Combine with tortellini. Toss well and marinate in refrigerator for 8-24 hours, tossing frequently.

Three hours before serving, remove salad from refrigerator and toss occasionally. Serve at room temperature garnished with parsley.

Nancy MacDonald

In the early spring when the ducks and geese are nesting — sometimes in our planter boxes — they also eat all our flowers and plants. It's so discouraging to come home in the evening and find all your plants just gone. They especially love lobelia and will nibble it down to stubble and then, as a final insult, pull out the dirt ball and leave it on the deck.

Jann McFarland

WINTER KIWI SALAD

2 kiwi fruit, peeled and sliced
1 banana, peeled and sliced diagonally
1 papaya, peeled, seeded and sliced

Honey-Lime Dressing:
2 T. vegetable oil
1 T. honey
1 T. lime juice
1/4 tsp. grated lime peel
1/8 tsp. paprika
Dash salt

Serves 4.

Combine kiwi, banana and papaya. Combine dressing ingredients and mix well. Toss fruit with dressing.

June Fauchald

"SLEEPLESS" VINAIGRETTE

Olive oil
Rice wine vinegar
Grey Poupon Dijon mustard
A healthy pinch of unhealthy white sugar or
   "healthy" raw sugar

Into a jar with a twist or screw cap (an empty Grey Poupon jar is perfect), pour about seven-eighths olive oil to one-eighth rice wine vinegar. Add the mustard (a level teaspoon for half a GP jar; a heaping teaspoon for more — exactly how much depends on your taste) and the sugar.

Put the cap on securely, and shake well for about a minute. You'll get a creamy yellow mixture.

Lesley Hazleton

Okay, so I know Nora Ephron has no idea how far it is from Lake Union to Alki Point*, but she sure knows one thing — that Grey Poupon mustard is the secret of a good vinaigrette (her recipe's at the end of her book, <u>Heartburn</u>). I have no idea why this should be. Neither does she. But since we all live within Grey Poupon distance of each other, it seems appropriate. This is based on Ephron's recipe, but quicker and easier. I once made this dressing in front of a French woman. She was appalled until she tasted it. "Do not tell anyone 'ow you did zis," she said. "Of course not," I promised....

*Note: The movie "Sleepless in Seattle", directed by Nora Ephron, was filmed on the dock next to Lesley's. She refers to one scene in which Tom Hanks' boat miraculously putts from Lake Union directly to Alki Point, miles away through the locks on Puget Sound!

GREEN GODDESS DRESSING

This recipe is from my mother who was a gourmet cook and greatly enjoyed cooking for her family and friends.

1 ripe avocado
1 cup mayonnaise
1/2 cup sour cream
1/4 cup tarragon vinegar
1/4 cup wine vinegar
1 small can rinsed drained anchovies
2 T. chopped green onions
1 T. lemon juice
1 clove garlic
Salt & pepper to taste

Makes 2 cups.

Mix all ingredients in blender. Chill 24 hours.

M. Liz Crowell

LAKE UNION OIL DRESSING

1 cup surface oil from water of Lake Union
1/4 cup oil scraped from bottom of steel-hulled vessel
1/4 cup oil from logs holding houseboat together
2/3 cup finely chopped Lake Union crawdads

Combine ingredients in a small bottle, shake well, mail to E.P.A.

Phil Webber

In the mid-1960's, the Floating Homes Association, in an effort to appease the City Council and answer complaints that houseboats were polluting Lake Union (though the lake sediment had been polluted years before by various manufacturing plants along the shores and is still polluted by outfall from the city sewer system), set about the unprecedented task of hooking each and every houseboat to the city sewer system. Nowhere in the world had this ever been done. In the Spring of 1967, the first houseboat dock was "plumbed", and the general upgrading of the houseboat community followed.
Houseboat Old-timer

Raccoons, Crawdads and Mallards

Meat, Seafood and Poultry

LEG OR SADDLE OF LAMB IN WINE

This recipe was translated from Hola!, a weekly magazine published in Spain. Art's houseboat is the meeting place of "Club Tango", a group of tango dancers and students. Usually a couple of belly dancers show up as well as Greeks, Yugoslavians and Argentineans, so they do a lot of different kinds of dancing besides the tango!

1 leg or saddle of lamb
2 wine glasses of tarragon vinegar (8 oz.)
2 wine glasses of olive oil (8 oz.)
4 cloves garlic, crushed
1 large onion, diced small
1 carrot, peeled and cut into round slices
1 bottle red wine
5 tomatoes, seeds removed and cut into large pieces
1 bay leaf
2 whole cloves
Salt to taste

Serves 6-8.

Marinate the lamb in a mixture of the oil, vinegar and carrot for 24 hours, leaving it in a cool place. In a casserole with a thick bottom, place the marinade liquid to heat and add the onions and the meat. Sprinkle with the wine and the tomatoes. Add bay leaf, cloves and salt. Allow it to cook slowly until you see that the meat begins to leave the bone. Then take it out and serve it with its gravy (put through a food processor or seive if desired) served in a separate gravy dish. Accompany with a green vegetable.

Art Hemenway

MARINATED BARBECUED LEG OF LAMB

Marinade:
1 cup dry red wine
3/4 cup soy sauce
6 large garlic cloves, crushed
1/2 cup fresh mint, chopped
1 T. bruised rosemary
1 T. black pepper

1 leg of lamb, approximately 6 lbs.

Serves 8-10

Have your butcher debone and butterfly the leg of lamb. Mix marinade ingredients and marinate the leg of lamb covered for at least 6 hours or overnight, turning frequently. Barbecue 12 minutes on one side, 10 minutes of the other side, for rare meat. Let stand 5 minutes covered with foil before carving.

Joan Hacker

"RACCOON" LAMB KABOBS

1 1/2 lbs. lean boneless lamb, cut into 1" cubes
2 medium onions
1 1/2 tsp. minced fresh garlic
2 T. fresh squeezed lemon juice
1 T. minced fresh oregano, or 2 tsp. dried
1/2 tsp. minced fresh rosemary, or 1/4 tsp. dried
1/3 cup dry white wine
3 T. olive oil, preferably extra virgin
2 T. red wine vinegar
1/4 tsp. salt
1/4 tsp. pepper
16 bay leaves
Slices of elephant garlic (optional)

Serves 4-6

For marinade, combine lemon juice, wine, olive oil, vinegar, garlic, oregano, rosemary, salt and pepper in large glass bowl and whisk until blended. Trim any fat and gristle from lamb and pat dry with paper towels. Add lamb to marinade and set aside to marinate at least 30 minutes.

Preheat grill (or can use broiler). Halve and peel onions. Cut lengthwise into wedges and separate wedges into sections 2 or 3 layers thick. Thread skewers alternately with lamb, onions, (elephant garlic slices) and bay leaves. Arrange skewers in single layer on grill. Brush generously with remaining marinade and cook lamb to desired doneness. Serve on Parsleyed Almond Rice (see recipe).

Becky and Mike Foley

While grilling kabobs one summer evening, I distinctly felt something fondling my bare toes. I glanced down and saw a small raccoon's foot sticking up through the decking with its paws groping over my foot. It was the young raccoon we had befriended that summer and he regularly showed up when the smell of food was in the air. (He especially liked to help me check the crawdad trap!)

MARY'S HOUSEBOAT GOURMET ROAST PORK

5 lb. loin of pork, boned
2 T. coarse salt
1 clove garlic
1/2 tsp. pepper
1/2 tsp. thyme

Serves 8.

Have a butcher bone the loin of pork. In a small bowl or mortar crush garlic clove with coarse salt and pepper and thyme. Rub the boned surface of the pork with the garlic mixture and let stand for at least 2 hours. Wipe off the garlic mixture, roll the roast, and tie it at 2" intervals with kitchen string. Put the pork in a pan and roast it in a pre-heated 450 F. oven for 30 minutes, then reduce heat to 350 F., and roast the pork for 2 hours or until a meat thermometer registers 185 F. Let the meat stand at room temperature until it is cool. Remove the string and arrange the roast, whole or cut into 1/4" slices, on a bed of "Roaring Rice Salad" on a platter. Serve with "Sailor's Sour Cherry Sauce" in little dipping cups. (See recipes.)

Mary Gey

I used this recipe for a dinner I had auctioned off at my daughter's school. It was an elegant affair. Before dinner our guests enjoyed appetizers on the deck, including some wonderful oysters and champagne. After the hors d'oeuvres, I noticed one gentleman standing in the kitchen sipping champagne and talking to his companion. Without paying much attention, he nonchalantly reached over to the countertop and scooped up a handful of Meow Mix kibble from the cat's dish, popped it in his mouth and chewed it up. I don't know what he thought he was eating but he never batted an eye, went right on chatting, then sat down for dinner!

2025 ROAST PIG

For 24 summers our houseboat dock has held a Bastille Day luau for friends and dock "alumni". We cook a pig in the ground, serve sangria and keg beer, smoked salmon and every guest brings a special potluck dish. We have a band and always a big turn out. The first few years we had diving contests, boat races, and other physically exerting events; now some people dance, and most of us (20 years later) would rather visit with friends, eat and drink. Here are a couple of our recipes. You will see a few others throughout the book.

Pig:
1 whole pig (approximately 150 lbs.) plus 2 legs (about 35 lbs.) — serves around 200-250 pig-outers. Have head and feet removed — takes up too much room in the pit. Bill Swain, who used to be the butcher at Pete's, will order whole pigs and deliver them (depending on where you live).

Spices:
2 large jars of Johnny's Seasoning Salt and all the fresh herbs you can snip from your neighbors' gardens -- mint, thyme, rosemary, oregano, sage, parsley, tarragon and basil. 2 boxes of old lettuce leaves from the grocery store (call ahead and order them).

Other "pig" items you will need:
10 feet of chicken wire (4 ft. wide), an old white bed sheet, 10 feet of burlap, about 20 feet of baling wire cut into 1 ft. lengths, wire cutters, and 8 to 10 clean bricks (wrapped in foil).

Further ingredients:
Pig carrier, beer, water hose, shovels, 4 meat hooks, old galvanized washtub, a gang of enthusiastic workers, strawberry daiquiris, a spot of ground for the pit (and permission to use it, we lean towards parking lots ourselves), fire permit, kindling and lots of alder logs, 100 bricks (more or less) to line the pig pit with, shopping cart, lawn chairs, picnic table, 4 pot holders, a cross, rubber gloves, several large pans or trays to serve the meat on, sharp knives, 3 or 4 wet towels, 2 saw horses, 2 large garbage cans lined with heavy duty garbage bags, and several people who like to play with their food (to carve).

Instructions:

2 weeks ahead, call everyone up and invite them; call Bill Swain at 282-5115 and order pig. 2 days before the party, dig pit: you will need a 6 to 8 ft. long by 4 ft. wide pit. Get several strong-armed men, plenty of beer and shovels, picks (depending if you are using a parking lot), jack hammer (if parking lot has cement). After pit is dug, it must be lined with bricks. You can use old bricks. Houseboaters are good scroungers. One year we all got in tippy canoes, kayaks, and old row-boats, and paddled over to the Gasworks Park to get bricks that some-one remembered seeing in about 2 or 3 feet of water over there. We filled our various water craft full of bricks and then tried to row back home. No one but houseboaters would be ridiculous enough to be out at night in canoes loaded with bricks...but anyway we got lots of bricks. When pit is done, stand around and slap everyone on the back, drink a little beer, and talk about how it gets harder to dig that pit out every year. Groan a lot about your trick back too. Put a board over pit so no one will drive their car into it.

1 day before the luau (i.e., for a Saturday 5 p.m. or so pig time, start this next part fairly early Friday morning), haul wood stolen from everybody on the dock's woodpiles in old shopping cart up to your pit. You will need piles and piles of wood. Be sure to have water hose by pit, as well as lawn chairs, and a supply of beer. Be sure all debris, bushes, etc. are cleared from around fire pit. Also, water the area around the pit and keep it damp all the time fire is going. Build huge fire in pit and feed it enough to keep it roaring for about 6 hours. A couple of people will probably call in to work sick to do fire duty. Sit in lawn chairs and drink a few beers. If kids are around, they can run errands, haul wood, etc. Around 3 p.m. or so switch to STRAW-BERRY DAIQUIRIS...someone will be home from work then and will volunteer to make them. You will need a very long extension cord and a blender, a bottle of rum, fresh strawberries, some cans of lemonade concentrate and lots of ice. Put all this in blender and liquefy. Will have to taste to get amount of lemonade concentrate right — don't use too much or it's too sweet. (Whole batches have been known to disappear during "tasting".)

During last hour or so before you put pig in, let the fire die down so that you have a bed of coals. While fire is dying down, have your foil-covered bricks in someone's oven at 500 F. They should heat for about 2 hours. You should now have your pig either picked up or delivered to the site.

One year when Bill the Butcher picked up the pig and put it in his truck to bring it over to the pit, he decided it would be really funny to lash the pig's head to the front of his pickup truck. As he drove up to a stop light, there was a Seattle Police car right next to him. Boy, was he sweating it that they would take it personally. Fortunately, they didn't. He said the next year he was going for a motorcycle (police) escort!

At one Pig Roast we were dancing to some good old rock 'n' roll provided by a band hired for the occasion. Couples danced all up and down the dock and on all the houseboat decks near the band. When one girl danced herself right into the lake, two guys came to her rescue, fished her out and kept right on dancing — never missed a beat!

Further Instructions:

Next, lay chicken wire over picnic table (the long way). Lay burlap in the middle over the chicken wire and the bed sheet on top of that. Pile lettuce leaves on bed sheet and branches of herbs on top of lettuce. Lay pig on top. Massage pig all over inside and out with seasoning salt and put rest of herbs inside of pig. Then get your hot bricks from the oven (using pot holders) and place them inside the pig (ouch!). Use as many as will fit. Cover pig generously with more of the lettuce leaves. Wrap sheet securely around pig — this is important because it keeps dirt from getting into the pig. Then wrap burlap tightly and secure with a few pieces of wire. To complete pig bundle, wrap chicken wire around pig and secure with the 12-inch pieces of wire. (Bet you forgot the wirecutters...better get some pliers, too, while you're at it, as our fingers are getting tender from twisting the wires.)

Pig is now ready to go in pit. Have pit crew shovel out hot coals into old wash tub (fill it up). Be sure to water down the whole surrounding area and keep it damp while you are doing this. Water the pig bundle a bit too before pitting it in the pit. Sometimes we have a brief water fight too. Pick your 4 strongest, soberest men to carry the pig to the pit using the 4 meat hooks hooked into pig bundle. Drop pig bundle carefully into pit — try not to lose footing and slip into pit with pig. Grab meat hooks back out, you'll need them tomorrow to get that sucker back out.

Immediately shovel the hot coals from the wash tub on top of pig. Kick the bricks around the edges of pit over on top of pig (collapse the pit onto pig). Shovel dirt over and stomp down. Hose down the pit area...Plant cross to mark grave. Can put inscription on if anyone has something clever to say. After all those daiquiris, you should be a real "ham". Cross will help you find your treasure tomorrow. Steam will probably be rising out of the ground. Let pig cook 24 hours.

When you are about 45 minutes from serving time, dig up pit — should still be hot so be careful. Put meat hooks through chicken wire again and lift onto pig carrier. Carry down dock with big parade of people cheering and cameras rolling. Place carrier on saw horses. (Be sure pig bearers are all the same height or else pig grease will start sliding to the low end of carrier resulting in a pig slick on the dock and then into the water and you will be cited by the EPA.)

And Finally:

Put lots of newspapers, plastic or whatever under the pig carrier and
unwrap pig. Frequently pig is so cooked you won't even need a knife
— just pull meat apart into serving size portions and plop onto trays. It
is usually quite hot. Hold a luau where everyone porks out. After all
meat is gone from the carcass, let school teachers take the funky backbone home for the kiddies to look at, dog lovers get a bone or two and
then let rest of it sit out overnight. (Cats will thank you in the morning
for letting them wade around up to their knees in pig grease all night.
And cat owners will thank you the next day when the greasy cats come
jump in bed with them in the morning.)

This recipe is pretty foolproof. The only times it has not worked, someone decided to take a shortcut and leave the bricks out of the pig or else
did not burn the pit long enough. (It really didn't matter though, we had
so much other food to eat!)

The 2025 Pit Crew

PORK & PEPPER STEW (LESKOVACKA MUCKALICA)

2 T. butter or margarine
2 T. vegetable oil
2 lbs. boneless pork, cut in 1/2" cubes
2 medium onions, sliced thin and separated into rings
2 T. flour
3 T. New Mexican red chile powder or hot Hungarian paprika
1 each, green, red and yellow bell peppers, cut into strips
2-3 Jalepeno or Serrano peppers (with seeds), fresh or canned, sliced into small rings
1 cup chicken stock
3 T. tomato paste
3 large garlic cloves, minced
1 bay leaf
1 tsp. salt

Serves 6.

Heat 2 tsp. of the butter and 2 tsp. of the oil together in a large pot. When the oil is very hot, add the pork in batches and brown on all sides, about 5 minutes. Remove pork. Add remaining butter and oil to the drippings in the pan. When hot, add the onions and cook them over medium heat, stirring frequently, until they are soft and golden colored. Sprinkle the flour and chile powder or paprika over the onions and cook for 2 minutes longer, stirring constantly. Reduce the heat and add the pork and the sliced peppers, chicken stock, tomato paste, garlic, salt and bay leaf. Stir to mix well. (There will seem to be not enough liquid in the mixture, but as the peppers cook they will release plenty of moisture.)

Increase the heat to bring the mixture to a boil. Then reduce heat to low, cover the pot, and let the stew simmer for 1 hour. Stir the mixture occasionally. Serve with lots of long grain white rice, a green salad, a side dish of thick yogurt, and hot cornbread — all washed down with cold beer or a strong red wine.

Jean Bakken

This stew (pronounced MOOCH-kah-leet-sa) is a specialty from the Serbian town of Leskovac. It's medium hot and is as good leftover as it is the first day.

86

Floating Homes Association

OVEN STEW

  1 1/2 lbs. beef, cubed
  8 carrots, sliced diagonally
  1 large onion, chopped
  1 cup celery, chopped
  2 cups potatoes, cubed
  2 cups tomato juice
  1 T. sugar
  3 T. tapioca
  2 cloves garlic, sliced
  1 tsp. soy sauce
  1 tsp. salt
  1/4 tsp. pepper
  1 T. Kitchen Bouquet

Serves 4-6.

Do not brown the meat. Mix all ingredients in a Dutch oven. Bake for 5-6 hours at 250 F. DO NOT OPEN THE OVEN.

Anna Brown

This tastes even better the second day.

*O*ur first houseboat was a tiny,

funky, old-fashioned one. We

loved it. A work colleague came to

pick me up one day. As I showed

her the house, I could see a

perplexed look. "If I lived here,"

she said, "I'd feel like I was on

vacation all the time!"

Ann Bassetti

COOKIN'-WHILE-YOU-PLAY BEEF BURGUNDY

2 lbs. cubed beef (round steak, sirloin, etc.)
1 can cream of mushroom soup (undiluted)
1 can cream of celery soup (undiluted)
1 envelope Lipton onion soup mix
1 cup Burgundy wine

Serves 8.

Brown beef in a casserole. Pour in both cans of soup. Sprinkle in dry soup and stir. Pour in wine and stir. (It looks like someone barfed, but don't be put off.) Cover and bake at 250 F. for 3 hours. Serve over noodles or rice.

Barbara & Dave Lefebvre

BBQ Brisket

    4-6 lbs. beef brisket (solid slab if possible)
    1 stalk celery
    1 medium onion
    2 cloves garlic (or to taste)
    2-4 oz. liquid smoke
    BBQ sauce (see recipe below)

Serves 8.

Purée celery, onion and garlic. Add liquid smoke. Spread the purée on the brisket and chill for 24 hours. Bake, covered, at 250 F. for 4-4 1/2 hours. For the last half hour of baking, scrape off the marinade and spread the brisket with a thick barbecue sauce. Continue baking, covered, for 1/2 hour. Let brisket cool a little before slicing thin.

Dawn Vyvyan

BBQ Sauce

    2 oz. butter
    1/4 cup olive oil
    1 cup chili sauce
    1/4 cup Worcestershire sauce
    2 tsp. paprika
    2 tsp. rosemary
    1 tsp. salt
    1 tsp. pepper
    1 tsp. cayenne pepper
    1 tsp. oregano
    2 tsp. chopped garlic

Makes 1 pint.

Mix all ingredients in the order listed.

Dawn Vyvyan

MINNIE'S MEOW MEAT BALLS

1 cup Minute Rice or regular rice
1 lb. hamburger
1 egg
2 tsp. grated onion
2 tsp. salt
Dash pepper
2 1/2 cups tomato juice or
    2 8 oz. cans tomato sauce + 1/2 cup water or
    whatever "tomato-y" liquids, i.e., salsa, bloody Mary mix
    to make 2 1/2 cups
1/2 tsp. sugar

Serves 6.

Mix rice, beef, egg, onion, salt, pepper and 1/2 cup of tomato juice lightly with your hands. Shape into 18 balls and place in skillet. Add sugar to remaining 2 cups of tomato juice. Pour juice over meatballs. Bring to a boil; then reduce heat and simmer, covered, for 15 minutes (or 20 minutes for regular rice).

Sandi McQuirk

GRANDMA'S HUNGARIAN BEEF

1 lb. sliced or stew cut beef
Pam spray or oil
1/2 cup chopped onion
1 clove garlic, minced
3/4 cup water
1/3 cup catsup
2 T. brown sugar
2 T. Worcestershire sauce
1/4 cup paprika
1 tsp. salt
1 tsp. brown mustard
1 tsp. cornstarch to thicken sauce

Serves 2-4

Sauté beef strips until brown. Add onions and garlic and sauté 3-5 minutes. Add 1/2 cup water, catsup, brown sugar, Worcestershire sauce, mustard, paprika and salt. Cover and simmer for 20 minutes. Mix remaining water with cornstarch and stir into beef. Heat and stir until thick and shiny. Serve over wide noodles or rice.

Michael & Bonnie Bell

Everything is flexible in this recipe. Modify time and ingredients to taste — I have for 20+ years, never using her recipe (Grandma's, that is) but always acknowledging her contribution. Don't forget a nice red wine — a touch in the sauce isn't bad either!

ALASKA MIKE'S MEATLOAF

1 lb. ground moosemeat, caribou, deer or hamburger
1 6 oz. pkg. onion soup mix
1 slice of bread, torn
1/2 cup milk
4 T. Alaska Mike's B.B.Q. sauce*

Serves 4.

Mix all ingredients together. Bake at 350 F. for 1 hour.

*Alaska Mike's B.B.Q. sauce is privately made. I'd give you the recipe, but I make it up every year. You can use a good quality home-made or store-bought sauce.

Mike McCrackin

*T*his recipe can be made in a
bread pan or free-formed loaf.
It's easy to make and very tasty.

HAMBURGER DAVE'S BBQ SECRETS

1 lb. hamburger
1 pkg. hamburger buns

Serves 1 cat, five ducks

When charcoal is appropriately hot, toss on hamburger patties. In the meantime, fix yourself a drink. After finishing drink, turn patties. Take a swim in the channel. Fix another drink. Walk to end of dock and watch lake activities. Return to grill and exclaim, "Where's the beef?" Feed miniature patties to your cat, the buns to the ducks, and head for the "318".

Dave Gardner

[Editor's note: The "318" is a tavern and burger joint on Westlake.]

When I graduated from high school I bought a houseboat on the ship canal, over by Foss Tug. A buddy moved in with me. We bought some cheap dishes at St. Vinnie's and set up housekeeping. I have to admit we weren't much good at the "keeping" part. The dishes stacked up day after day in the sink. After a month or so they'd be so disgusting that we couldn't stand to wash them. Our solution was to take the whole stack down the dock and skip the plates one by one across the water, trying to hit the ducks! I'm embarrassed to admit we actively sought out ducks to aim at. Then back to St. Vinnie's for a new load of (clean) dishes!

Gary Seese

PORTAGE BAY BULLFROG BROIL

When I was a kid, my brother and I would catch big bull frogs along the banks of Portage Bay. One time we put several in the refrigerator to see what would happen. When my Mom opened the door, there were those big old bull frogs sitting in the middle of her jello salad. (I'm surprised I lived to tell about it!)

Sid McFarland

4 large bullfrog legs
1 T. soy sauce
1/4 tsp. garlic paste
1/4 cup vermouth, warmed
Lemon herb spice mix
Houseboat water weeds
Juice of 1/2 lemon

Serves 3 hungry cats or 1 unsuspecting guest.

Skin bullfrog legs. Combine soy sauce, garlic paste and warm vermouth and marinate legs. Remove from marinade, sprinkle lightly with lemon herb mix and wrap loosely in houseboat water weeds (preferably without outboard motor fuel/oil mix). Soak in lemon juice. Wrap in aluminum foil and broil for 15 minutes, turning once. Serve with brown rice and green beans julienne. Precede with caesar salad with anchovies. For dessert: raspberry sherbet smothered with whipped cream and almonds.

Dick McMillen

BOUDIN

3 hanks small sausage casing
1 lb. cooked chicken breast meat
1 lb. lean pork cut in chunks
1 lb. pork fat cut in chunks
3 cups chopped onions
2/3 cup minced fresh parsley
12 garlic cloves, chopped
1/2 cup chopped green onion tops
2 cups heavy cream
1/2 cup water
6 cups cooked long grain white rice
1 T. sage
5 tsp. salt
3/4 tsp. fresh ground pepper
2 tsp. cayenne (more or less to taste)
1/3 tsp. ground bay leaf
1/2 tsp. thyme
Dash allspice
1/8 tsp. mace

Serves 6-8 "Ragin' Cajuns"

Wash salt out of casings by running water through them. Let soak in water for 1 hour. Rinse. Grind all meat and vegetable ingredients with meat grinder or food processor and put in large mixing bowl. Add cooked rice and spices and start mixing with your hands. Put through grinder again. Add cream to bind stuffing together. Add the water only if needed. Begin stuffing into 8" lengths of casings with sausage press or meat grinder attachment. Tie off links with string if necessary. Freeze until ready to cook. Cook boudin in a frying pan with a little water on low heat for about 20 minutes. Don't let pan get too hot or the heat will break the casings. Serve with whiskey and good Cajun music. Poo Yieii!

Bob West

I used to make boudin at Pete's Super Market, our neighborhood store, many years ago. It was sold around the holidays as a special treat. It's good stuffed in turkey too. The Cajun people around Mamou and Basile, Louisiana, know how to begin a Saturday morning. I found that out at Fred's Lounge during a morning radio broadcast of live Cajun music. On hand always is hot boudin and whiskey. Boudin looks like sausage but is actually a rice dressing with greens and meat. (The whiskey looked like whiskey anywhere, but I had to try it out anyway!)

ERMA RUTH'S CHICKEN FRIED STEAK WITH COUNTRY CREAM GRAVY

Chicken fried steak must be on the menu of every "down-home" greasy spoon cafe in West Texas (and points north, south, east and west of there). Jim's sister-in-law, Erma Ruth, showed me how to make it when she visited one summer. She also tried to show me how to make greens, but they always seemed to taste like spinach, so I substitute frozen peas.

4 cube (or minute) steaks
1 egg
1 qt. milk
1 cup flour
Paprika
Salt and pepper to taste
Cooking oil

Serves 4.

Heat oil in skillet or electric frying pan (300 F.). Wash steaks under running water. (I've never been sure this is essential, but I do it anyway.) Put flour on a 10" plate. Mix egg and 1/4 cup of the milk in a bowl with a fork. Dip meat in egg/milk mixture. Salt and pepper both sides of meat. Then pat meat in the flour. Place in hot oil and fry until brown, then turn (about 10 minutes for the first side and 5-10 minutes for the second). Remove meat to paper towels over foil and wrap loosely around meat to keep warm.

Gravy: Pour off all oil but about 1/4 cup. Add 1/4 cup or so of the flour left on the plate and brown in the oil. Gradually add 2-3 cups of milk, stirring constantly, until thick. Salt and pepper to taste. Gravy will be light in color (heavy in calories). Add paprika for color if you like. Serve with mashed 'taters and greens.

Linda Knight

REAL TEXAS BARBECUE

5 lbs. beef brisket
"Classic Coke" or your favorite beer (not "lite"), enough to cover brisket
Brisket rub (Fiesta Brand)
Garlic salt
Course ground pepper
Lemon pepper
Barbecue sauce (your own or a commercial brand)

Weber-type barbecue with tight fitting lid
Mesquite or hickory chips

Serves 6

Marinate brisket overnight in the Coke or beer. Remove from marinade and rub with Brisket Rub. Sprinkle generously with seasonings. Fire up the charcoal, and when coals are white, sprinkle them with the pre-soaked mesquite or hickory chips. Use the leftover Coke or beer in the smoker pan under the meat. Keep adding liquid as needed. Turn meat and baste with pan drippings and barbecue sauce about every hour. Proper cooking in the average barbecue takes two cycles; you should baste and use the Brisket Rub with the meat off the fire while the second batch of coals is burning down. Cooking time is about 4-5 hours.

Dave and Marty Gardner

Some wonderful San Antonio friends pay us a visit most every year and are happy to bring a sort of entry fee for the privilege — Real Texas Barbecue. Every visit they dutifully hand-carry some 5-6 pounds of Texas barbecued brisket in order to gain entrance to our house. (They're paid back in fresh salmon, of course.) Upon their arrival we politely greet them, snatch the brisket (the knife and napkins are already on the table), and begin devouring this scrumptious treat!

One summer, residents of Mallard Cove decided to don old aloha shirts, grass skirts, flowers and muumuus to celebrate a floating Luau. We gathered together five or more large floats in front of the Hainer's houseboat, rented a palm tree, and turned up the Hawaiian music. Theresa gave hula lessons while Kay roasted the Kalua pig, barbecued the fish, and concocted the Mai Tais. The party started in midafternoon and lasted into the balmy moonlit evening. We danced the hula even as we returned the last float with its lone palm tree to its own moorage in front of the Hendrickson's houseboat. It's amazing what the rental of one palm tree can inspire. Without an imu (pit) to roast the pua'a (pig) in, houseboaters must improvise. The following is a recipe for Hawaiian Pua'a without the imu.

HOUSEBOAT KALUA PIG

5 lbs. pork butt or shoulder
5 cloves garlic, finely diced
1/2 cup vinegar
1 1/2 tsp. Liquid Smoke
Ti leaves (very inexpensive from Uwajimaya;
    may substitute aluminum foil, but will sacrifice aesthetics)
2 tsp. pepper
Rock salt

Serves 8-10

Mix vinegar, garlic, Liquid Smoke and pepper in wooden bowl. Make several punctures into the pork with a sharp knife. By hand, push some of the mixture into the slits in the pork, and marinate overnight, or at least for several hours, in refrigerator. Just before baking in oven, wrap the pork roast tightly with several ti leaves and skewer. Place directly in roasting pan and bake at 300 F. for 3 hours.

Now this is the most important part: For authentically served kalua (steamed) pig, NEVER, NEVER slice the cooked pork. ALWAYS hand strip the pork with the grain to retain moisture in the meat. This is the way Hawaiians do it to this day, usually keeping a bucket of cool water next to the "Stripper", who alternates between cooling his fingers in the bucket and stripping the steaming pork from the succulent pig. The pua'a is served in long strips, sprinkled with rock salt. This is very "onolicious," as they say in the islands, and is much tastier than "meataloafa." Serve with poi, fresh fruit and "Lomi Lomi Salmon" (see recipe).

Theresa Jones, transplanted Hawaiian

LOMI LOMI SALMON

1 1/2 lbs. fresh or salted salmon
4 firm ripe medium sized tomatoes
1 medium Maui or Walla Walla sweet onion
1 scallion

Serves 8-10

Debone and remove skin from salmon. Dice salmon, tomatoes and onion. Combine and chill. Just before serving, toss lightly with a few ice cubes to keep moist and cool. Serve in wooden bowl. Sprinkle diced scallion (including green) on mixture.

This should be served at every Floating Luau!

Theresa Jones

One may wonder what it is about Lake Union and Hawaiian traditions. Two houseboat coops have pig roast events and the Duck Dodge has an annual Hawaiian night race, replete with palm trees on the shrouds and sailors in grass skirts. Maybe it's the water...?

HOUSEBOAT SMOKEY SALMON

Fresh salmon
Salt
Brown sugar

Select unfrozen salmon (frozen tends to be dry and break apart). Buy fillets or remove entire backbone and cut into any size pieces with or without skin (the skin tends to hold the pieces together). Ideal size is about 3 to 4 inches. The best way would be to cut one complete side of salmon into 3 to 5 pieces. The smaller the pieces, the easier they are to get off the grill without breakage.

In a large container, place enough water to cover the amount of salmon you have. Dissolve salt into the water until saturated. Dissolve 1/2 to 1 lb. of brown sugar in the salt solution. Place salmon in this brine for 12 to 24 hours. Before cooking, remove from brine and rinse off in running water for 15 minutes.

Use an outdoor barbecue that can be covered; build an extra large fire of charcoal. When red hot, place large chips of green alder (or cherry, hickory, etc.) on top of coals. Place fish on grill and cover. Vent just enough so that there is more smoke than heat. Cook for about 15 minutes — serve hot or room temperature. Note: If salt crystals form upon cooling, extend the rinsing period after soaking in the brine.

Each year we serve 75 pounds of this smoked salmon at the 2025 Bastille Day Luau. Sid and helpers smoke the salmon on our houseboat deck, and over the years salmon lovers know to wander down to the "source" for nibbles before the platter is formally presented at the Luau — with the few small pieces that were not already consumed by the tasting committee!

Sid McFarland

Our cat, Max, was about a year old at his first Luau. After the food was served, he "disappeared" and when we finally found him he was running back and forth across two houseboat roofs begging for salmon bites from everyone in the food line. For the next several days he would drag out old hunks of salmon he had stashed away.

"SLIME CITY HANDICAP" BLACKENED SALMON

1 salmon, filleted, skinned and cut into 2" x 3" pieces
Melted butter
Paul Prudhomme's "Magic Seasoning Blend"

1 lb. of fish serves 3.

Dip salmon pieces in butter. Sprinkle them liberally with the seasoning. Cook them until blackened in a VERY HOT cast iron skillet.

Sheri Lockwood and Chris Nowicki

The hit of the 1993 Fourth of July Party and 1st Annual "Slime City Handicap" Slug Races was this recipe for blackened salmon. The slug races were held in the parking lot on a big plasticized archery target and we had five heats to choose the races for the main event. No one was admitted without a racing slug, and as the slugs were to be put out to stud in the wilds after the races, no slugicide was allowed. The name of this recipe probably won't appeal to too many eager eaters, but it's easy and delicious. Be careful, though. Smoke was pouring out the doors and windows and it looked like the house was on fire, so it's probably best to do this outside on the barbecue!

We houseboaters are so lucky to have these plentiful beasties living in Lake Union. There are many ways to lure them to your table. A piece of salami tied to a weighted string works fine. We've also been able to nab ones near the surface with a pair of kitchen tongs and fast reflexes. The best method, though, is a wooden crawfish trap.

I put cat food in a stainless steel tea-ball for bait. Put the trap down in the evening and harvest in the morning. Put back all egg-bearing females (you can see eggs attached near underside of tail). I put newly caught log lobsters in a bucket of fresh tap water, and cover with a weighted grate (to keep critters out), and leave for at least 12 hours. This cleans crawdads of any "muddy-lake" taste.

LOG LOBSTERS (CRAWFISH)

10 crawfish per person
1 cube of unsalted butter
1 T. minced fresh parsley
1/4 tsp. Johnny's All-Purpose Seasoning
1 T. lemon juice

I still cringe every time I grab one of these squirmy fellers and chuck him into a large pot full of boiling water, but that's the best way, so they say. Anyway, add one lemon, sliced in half, to water. I do about 6 crawfish at a time. Boil for 8 minutes. Then plunge into ice-water for a minute and let drain on paper toweling. If you do not have enough to serve, put them in a zip-lock bag and freeze for future use.

You can cook and present these beautiful log lobsters in many delightful ways, but my favorite is the most simple and, I think, most eye-appealing.

Melt butter over low heat. Add parsley, Johnny's Seasoning and lemon juice. Serve the crawfish, cold, piled decoratively on a platter. Break off tails and claws, discard body. Pull shell and legs off tail. Dip into butter and fly off to heaven.

Melanie Hester

CRAWFISH SOUFFLÉ

1/4 cup butter
Parmesan cheese
1/4 cup flour
Pinch salt
1 cup milk
4 eggs, separated
1/2 tsp. cream of tartar seasoning
4 oz. shelled crayfish (other fish or crabmeat optional)
1/2 cup Swiss cheese
1 T. onion, diced

Serves 4.

Butter soufflé dish and dust with Parmesan. In pan melt 1/4 cup butter. Blend in flour and salt, and cook until bubbly. Stir in milk. Cook and stir until it boils and is smooth and thick. In bowl beat egg whites with cream of tartar until stiff. Shell crawfish, keeping only the tails. (Save the heads as bait for more crawfish.) Blend egg yolks, crawfish, Swiss cheese and onion into pan sauce. Fold this into egg whites. Pour into baking dish. Bake at 350 F. for 40 minutes until puffy and brown.

Laurie Lorence

This is a home-caught, home-cooked recipe. We've always fished for crawfish right off our back porch with homemade traps, and everyone gets into the act — including our cat, Emma. She reaches down onto the logs and snatches the ferocious beasts, bringing them in as presents. One receiver of these thoughtful gifts was our housesitter. We called home one day expecting to hear that all was well, but instead received a frantic reply to our "How's everything?" question. "There's a creature crawling on your sofa", she wailed, "and I think it escaped from your fishbowl! Should I put it back?"

Mike Zylstra (who has now moved away from houseboat living) first attempted this dish as a contribution to a "husbands cook" potluck. He was adamant about preparing "Crawdad Zylstra" without any help or advice from me. After an hour of kitchen noises, I heard a cry of "Help, this sauce won't thicken." I had difficulty controlling my rising laughter as I watched him vigorously trying to stir cold milk, lumpy flour, and chunks of butter into a smooth sauce in a mixing bowl. Mike was using an old family recipe which a seasoned cook had copied in cooking shorthand. The directions simply said, "make a white sauce of butter, flour and milk." After I explained the use of heat as an important element in achieving a thick white sauce, he started again and prepared a four-star casserole. The next day, Mike rewrote the recipe after some rouxed research in The Joy of Cooking.

CRAWDAD ZYLSTRA [OR MIKE'S ROUXED AWAKENING]

1/3 cup flour
1/3 cup melted butter
3 cups milk
6 oz. sharp cheese, shredded
dash pepper
2/3 cup brown rice (uncooked)
1/2 tsp. curry powder
1/2-1 lb. cooked fresh crawdads or shrimp
1/2 cup fine bread crumbs

Serves 4-5

Cook brown rice.

Make a roux by slowly stirring flour into melted butter. Blend over low heat for 3 to 5 minutes. Add milk and stir while heating until thick. Remove from heat and add shredded sharp cheese and a dash of pepper.

Combine rice with roux in a large mixing bowl and add curry powder dissolved in 1 T. hot water. Stir in cooked fresh crawdads (or cooked fresh shrimp). Pour into greased casserole and top with fine bread crumbs. Cook 30 to 40 minutes at about 350 F. or until bubbly.

Jewel Bergen-Brumbaugh

DECK HOPPER'S SPICY STEAMED BLACK COD

1 1/2 to 2 lbs. black cod fillets
1 T. dry sherry
1/2 tsp. salt
2 T. minced bacon
1 T. fermented black beans
1-1 1/2 tsp. chili powder
1 T. minced garlic
4 to 6 1/8" slices ginger root
1 T. vegetable oil
2 T. soy sauce
2 green onions (2" pieces)

Serves 4.

Score the fillets and rub with sherry and salt. Place fish on steaming dish and cover with rest of the ingredients. Steam for approximately 10 to 15 minutes until fish flakes with a fork.

Steve Hansen

Truly talented deck hoppers land on Steve Hansen's deck when they catch a whiff of his glorious Chinese dinners.

NORTHWEST BOUILLABAISSE

1 28 oz. can of whole tomatoes
2 leafy tops of celery stalks, chopped in 1" pieces
2 medium-sized onions, coarsely chopped
7 to 8 cloves of garlic
2 cups white wine
2 cups chicken stock
Juice of 1 orange and a little grated peel
1 lb. halibut or cod, cut in 1" slices
2 lb. salmon fillets, cut in 1" slices
2 lb. shrimp or crawdads (pre-cooked and cleaned)
2 dozen butter clams or mussels (in the shells)
2 cracked crabs (in the shell, pre-cooked and cleaned)
1 T. salt
1 T. tarragon (or, for a change, rosemary)
1 tsp. pepper
2 T. brown sugar
1 loaf French bread, sliced in 2" slices
Grated Parmesan or Gruyère cheese

If the folks in Marseille hadn't invented it first, we would have had to.

Serves 10.

Get a BIG kettle. Put in the tomatoes, onion, celery, wine, garlic, orange juice and gratings. On medium heat bring to a boil, then reduce heat until it's simmering. Add the halibut and salmon. Add all the seasonings. Simmer for about a half hour. Add a little water occasionally during simmering to keep it soupy. Add the rest of the seafood (including the shells). Heat long enough to bring to a simmer and warm the shellfish through. Remove seafood to a platter, leaving soup. Sprinkle the Parmesan or Gruyère on the bread slices and toast under the broiler until golden. Put bread slices in soup bowls, pour soup over top, and serve. Serve seafood on platter with extra plates and hammers (for shells).

Beth Means

TUB OF MUSSELS

1 T. butter
1 T. chopped shallot or onion
1 T. parsley
1 1/2 quarts of mussels, well scrubbed
1/2 cup white wine
1/2 cup butter
Lemon juice
Salt and pepper to taste
1/2 tsp. flour

In a saucepan place 1 T. butter, shallots, parsley and any additional herbs and spices you wish. Add the mussels and wine, and cook over high heat for 5 minutes or until shells are opened wide. Remove the mussels from the pan. Reduce the liquid in the pan over high heat to 1/3 of its original quantity. Add the 1/2 cup butter, lemon juice and salt and pepper. Pour sauce over mussels in their shells. You may thicken the sauce if your wish with the flour added to the butter before it is combined with the reduced sauce.

Laurie and Keith Lorence

It was the bathroom's turn in the never-ending process of remodeling our houseboat. Having chosen a modern shower enclosure to replace our pseudo-antique, declawed bathtub, we found ourselves in a quandary as to what to do with this well-loved family member. Rather than consign it to the landfill, we decided to give it to a neighbor who lived up the lake. We carefully loaded the tub onto our boat, the drain hole plugged with a customized potato. Our small sailboat leaned precariously as it navigated the hazardous channel. In the middle of the Great Lake Union, we eased the trusting structure over the side, intending to tow it for the rest of the voyage. Instead, we watched in horror as it immediately slipped beneath the icy waves, the traitorous spud floating away safely. To quote a famous yachtsman, "She went down like a greased safe!"

We prepared oysters this way several years ago at a dock potluck and the only thing I'd do differently is to fire up two BBQ's and space them strategically along the dock. We were all so anxious for these oysters that we had gathered around the one BBQ. So intent upon oyster eating were we that no one noticed the dock was sinking until the lake came lapping at our ankles! Things got exciting there for a couple of minutes, but balance was restored and the party rocked on. As I recall, that was the same dock party where the police officer who came to quiet us down a couple of times joined the party after he got off duty. But that's another story....

TENAS CHUCK BBQ OYSTERS

2 buckets of fresh oysters in the shell
1 (or 2) hot BBQ's with grill set several inches above coals

Serves: The whole dock!

Remove any rocks from the outside of the oysters (they tend to blow up when heated) and place them on the grill. When the oyster is done, the shell opens with a "phssst" and can then be opened the rest of the way with tongs and an oyster knife. If a particularly large oyster needs more cooking, it can be placed back onto the grill on the half shell until done. Serve with bowls of dipping sauces such as horseradish, cocktail sauce, melted butter or salsa.

Mary Gosslee

Tui Tui Cioppino

1/4 cup olive or salad oil
1 large onion, chopped
2 cloves garlic, minced or pressed
1 large green pepper, seeded and chopped or
    1 or 2 hot jalapeno peppers
1/3 cup chopped parsley
1 can (15 oz.) tomato sauce
1 can (1 lb. 12 oz.) tomatoes
1 cup dry red or white wine
1 bay leaf
1 tsp. dry basil
1 tsp. oregano leaves
1 dozen fresh clams in shells
1 lb. medium-sized raw shrimp
2 large Dungeness crabs, cleaned and cracked
Lake Union crawdads in whatever quantity you can find
Any other fresh seafood that you enjoy

Serves 6.

In a large kettle (at least 6 quarts) heat the oil over medium heat. Add the onion, garlic, green and/or jalapeno pepper and parsley. Cook, stirring often, until the onion is soft. Stir in the tomato sauce, tomatoes and their liquid, breaking up tomatoes, and the wine, bay leaf, basil and oregano. Cover and simmer until slightly thickened.

Meanwhile, scrub the clams to remove any sand. Shell and clean shrimp and crab. Add seafood. Cover and simmer gently about 20 minutes or until clams pop open and shrimp turn pink. Serve in bowls or soup plates with sour dough French bread and plenty of napkins.

Janet Yoder and Robert Rudine

The tiny sovereign nation of the Archipelago and Greater Tui Tui of the Joyous Lake has been fully independent since December 16, 1985. The Archipelago itself consists of two permanently inhabited floating islands: the capital isle of Grande Tui and the autonomous Isle Regis. The number of other islets depends on the vagaries of the lockmaster's lacustrine tides. The nation is a member since 1987 of the International Council of Independent States. Tui Tui has issued stamps since 1983 during its colonial period. Many of the stamp issues feature our country's coat of arms: Hexagram Tui escutcheoned on a shield surmounted by bumbershoot splendant, flanked by crawdads rampant and enscrolled with the motto: "Hyas kloshe hyas spose wake snass." The motto translates from the Chinook Jargon, "It's mighty nice, supposin' it don't rain."

Houseboaters all know that, except for some crawdads, Lake Union doesn't exactly offer much of a selection for the gourmet seafood lover. Perhaps guppy stew or an occasional minnow. But Tom and Peggy Stockley feasted on a lovely 16-inch rainbow trout one evening several years ago and they didn't even have to fish for it. The story (and they have witnesses, so stop rolling your eyes) goes like this:

Tom returned home from work one autumn afternoon to hear splashing out near the back deck. He went out to investigate. A trout was swimming back and forth frantically in the rowboat which was filled with rainwater. The trout had apparently jumped out of the water and directly into the boat! The neighbors denied any practical jokes.

(cont'd next page)

CILANTRO SHRIMP

24 large shrimp, peeled and deveined (1 1/2 lbs.)
1 T. Southwest Seasoning (recipe follows)
3/4 cup Cilantro Oil (recipe follows)
1/4 cup chopped green onions
1/4 cup chopped red bell peppers

Serves 4.

Sprinkle the shrimp with the Southwest Seasoning and use your hands to coat thoroughly. Heat a large, heavy dry skillet over high heat. When the skillet is very hot, add the shrimp and sear them for 3 minutes on each side or until they appear cooked through. Remove from heat.

To serve, spoon 2 tablespoons of the Cilantro Oil onto each of 4 plates. Arrange 6 shrimp on top and drizzle with another tablespoon of the oil. Sprinkle each serving with 1 tablespoon of the green onions and 1 tablespoon of the red bell peppers.

Jean Bakken

SOUTHWEST SEASONING

    2 T. chili powder
    2 T paprika
    1 T. ground coriander
    1 T. garlic powder
    1 T. salt (or to taste)
    2 tsp. ground cumin
    1 tsp. cayenne pepper
    1 tsp. crushed red pepper
    1 tsp. black pepper
    1 tsp. dried leaf oregano

Makes approximately 1/2 cup.

Combine all ingredients thoroughly and store in an airtight jar or container.

CILANTRO OIL

    1/2 cup PACKED cilantro leaves
    1 tsp. minced shallots
    1 tsp. minced garlic
    1/2 tsp. salt
    3 turns fresh ground pepper
    3/4 cup olive oil

Makes 3/4 cup.

Combine all ingredients in a food processor or blender and purée about 1 minute. Store in the refrigerator in an airtight jar or bottle for up to 1 week.

Jean Bakken

When Peggy returned from work (most of the dock had gathered by then), there was a lengthy discussion about the fate of the poor fish. Peggy wanted to set it free, but was booed down. Tom's suggestion won out — clean the fish and fire up the grill. Brushed with a little lemon butter, it made a delicious dinner and Tom's been checking the rowboat ever since!

Tom & Peg Stockley

Cioppino

1 1/2 lbs. boned sea bass, cut in 2 inch pieces
   (or any solid white fish such as halibut or
   turbot or swordfish; sole and snapper are
   too tender to hold together)
3 - 1 1/2 lb. lobsters, cut up (or 6 medium lobster tails)*
12-20 clams, depending on size, well scrubbed
20 mussels, well cleaned and scrubbed
1 lb. prawns, shelled
2 Dungeness crab, cleaned, cracked and broken up
2 cups chopped onion
1/2 cup chopped green pepper
1/2 cup chopped carrot
3 cloves garlic, crushed
8 cloves garlic, minced
1/2 cup olive oil
1 can (2 lb. 3 oz.) Italian tomatoes with basil
1 6 oz. can tomato paste
3 cups red wine
1 lemon, sliced thin
1 cup parsley, chopped
1/2 cup fresh basil, chopped (or 2 tsp. dried)
2 tsp. oregano
1 T. mild chili powder
1/2 tsp. salt
Fresh coarse-ground black pepper
6 whole cooked prawns for garnish
Plenty of garlic bread or toast

Serves 6

Combine onion, green pepper, carrots and minced garlic with olive oil in really large stock pot or kettle. Cook over low heat for 10 minutes, stirring occasionally. Add tomatoes, tomato paste, wine, lemon, 1/2 of the parsley, and rest of seasonings, except the crushed garlic. Bring to boil, reduce heat, cover and simmer for 20 minutes. Add bass, lobsters and shrimp and simmer, covered, for 20 minutes. Add clams, mussels and crushed garlic and simmer for about 10 minutes.

Most of the work required for this is chopping, all of which can be done ahead of time and ingredients stored in tightly covered containers. Serve the cioppino from the big pot it was cooked in. One good way to serve it is to put a round of garlic bread at the bottom of each bowl to serve as a blotter. After cioppino, guests should be provided with finger bowls, warm moist cloth napkins or paper towels, depending on how formal you are, or hot showers and huge fluffy bath towels, depending on how messy they are.

Serve in wide soup bowls using ladle and tongs. Sprinkle each bowl with parsley and garnish with a large unshelled prawn on top.

For super garlic toast, melt 1/4 lb. butter and crush therein 4 cloves garlic. Slice Italian (or French) bread about 3/4 inch thick, brush with butter-garlic mixture and sprinkle liberally with freshly grated, imported Romano cheese. Place slices on baking sheet, place under broiler and watch like an eagle until it's golden — the toast, not the eagle!

Art Hemenway

* If you find the lobster too rich for your pocketbook, just use more of the other seafoods.

BEIJING DUCK VIA HO CHI MINH CITY

In 1952 many houseboats were occupied by starving students. Houseboats were a good housing choice because the community was within walking distance of the UW and rent was cheap. A certain student, who is now a Seattle executive, lived with two friends in a rundown houseboat on Lake Union. When this young fellow saw how bold the Canada Geese were, a little light bulb lit up in his head. On his next weekend home at his family's farm, he picked up a small sack of chicken feed corn and brought it back to the houseboat.

(cont'd next page)

1 domestic duck, dressed

Sauce:
1/2 cup honey
1/2 cup water
1 T. soy sauce

Condiments:
Rice paper sheets
Cilantro leaves
Grated carrot
Pickled onion
Lettuce
Bean sprouts
Plum sauce (hoisin)
Chopped unsalted peanuts
Sweetened rice vinegar and chili sauce

Serves 2.

Scald duck for 10 seconds in boiling water to cover. Hang duck over sink with electric fan playing on duck until skin is dry and paper-like.

Combine the honey, water and soy sauce and paint duck with this mixture. Blow dry between coats until all the sauce is used up.

Roast duck on rack in preheated 450 F. oven for 25 minutes. Reduce heat to 350 F. and cook 55 minutes. Turn heat back up to 450 F. until juices run transparent.

Serve small portions of crisp skin with meat, rolled up in rice paper sheets softened in warm water. Accompany with condiments and dunk in sauce of sweetened rice vinegar and chili sauce.

Anonymous

WOODSTOVE GAME HEN

1 Cornish game hen (per person)
1 tsp. butter
1 T. soy sauce (optional)*
1 T. white wine (optional)*
2 sheets aluminum foil, each 3 feet long (one of these preferably heavy duty)

Serves 1 person per bird

Crinkle the aluminum sheets lightly to help heat distribution. Place heavy sheet on the table first, with light sheet on the top. Place washed bird on the end of the sheet. Add butter, soy, and wine. Roll bird in top sheet, tucking in ends. Roll package in second sheet, tucking in ends.

The fire in your woodstove may be hours old and very hot, or recently started and still low. It makes no difference; just place the wrapped bird directly on logs or coals, leaving the stove door open. Turn every 10 or 15 minutes. Cook for 40 minutes (very hot fire) or for 60 minutes (very low fire). When done cooking, spread newspapers four feet across the floor. Place package on newspapers and unwrap. If cooking several birds, unwrap just one first to see if it is done.

*Butter without soy or wine gives a crispier bird.

John Pursell

Soon a few geese were making it a habit to have a snack on the student's deck every evening. Each day he would spread the corn a little closer to his open door. At last a goose stepped in through the open door. Slam! Wring neck! Pluck! Dress! Roast! Eat! The wages of this sin were not only that the meat was tough and stringy, but that until they moved out in June, every step taken in that house would whuff up great billowing clouds of inescapable goose down!

Anonymous

BRAISED "LAUGHING" DUCK

1 fresh duck
3/4 cup soy sauce
10 cups vegetable oil
2 1/8" slices of ginger (crushed)
2 green onions
1/2 tsp. Chinese five-spice powder
3 T. dry sherry
1/2 T. brown sugar
8 cups of chicken broth (or water)
1 1/2 tsp. salt
1 1/2 lbs. spinach, washed, stems removed
1 T. minced parsley

Serves 2.

Marinate the duck in the soy sauce for 45 minutes. Drain the duck and reserve the soy sauce. Heat the oil in a wok until very hot. Deep fry the duck for 10 minutes, turning it every two minutes until brown. Drain the duck.

Put the duck in a pot. Add ginger, onions, five-spice powder, sherry, sugar, chicken broth, salt, and the reserved soy sauce. Bring to a boil, then reduce heat and simmer for 2 to 2 1/2 hours. Remove duck to serving platter. Leave gravy in the pot, skim off grease, then add the spinach and increase heat until the liquid bubbles. Cook until the spinach wilts. Remove the spinach and place it on the platter around the duck. Sprinkle the parsley over the duck and pour the gravy over all.

Steve Hansen

If you've ever listened to the cackle of our feathered neighbors as they march across your deck, usually at 5:00 a.m., you know why we call this "laughing" duck.

HOUSEBOATERS' SPICY CHICKEN WITH SUMMER VEGETABLES

Marinade:
1/2 cup olive oil
1 tsp. sesame oil
2 tsp. lemon juice
1/4 tsp. ground coriander
1/4 tsp. ground cinnamon
Pinch ground cumin
Pinch turmeric
1/2 tsp. ginger juice
Pinch paprika
Pinch cayenne pepper
Pinch ground cloves
1/4 tsp. kosher salt

10 chicken breasts (half breasts)
10 leeks
6 red bell peppers
30 new potatoes (small)
6 yellow bell peppers
4 crushed garlic cloves
1/4 cup lemon juice
Salt and pepper
1/2 cup chopped fresh basil
10 whole basil leaves

*F*or entertaining on the deck you can't beat this great early summer dish which makes use of seasonal ingredients and is colorful as well as easy to prepare. It makes a complete meal along with bread and salad.

Serves 8-10

For marinade, warm oil and add mixed spices to oil. Cool marinade.

Toss chicken breasts in cooled marinade and let sit for 3-4 hours. Halve red and yellow peppers, remove seeds and set aside. Halve new potatoes and steam until *al dente*.

Cut leeks just above white stem and clean thoroughly. Toss peppers, leeks and new potatoes in lemon juice, salt, pepper and garlic. Grill all ingredients over mesquite charcoal and watch carefully to prevent over charring of vegetables and chicken. Present on a large platter, sprinkle basil over vegetables and garnish with whole basil leaves.

Don Smith

CIRC SAW TURKEY AND THE TURKEY DUST SAGA

One night a bunch of us were sitting around sipping a few gin & tonics in an older houseboat, when there was a knock on the door. It was Mike Redman. He introduced himself and explained that he had lived in that houseboat some years back. So, of course, we invited him in, gave him a drink, and immediately began asking questions about his adventures living down here. We mentioned we were working on a cookbook and he told this story amid much hooting and laughter. He left (hours later) promising to write the story/recipe down and send it to us. We thought, "Oh, sure, he'll never remember." Lucky for us he did!

Many years ago, oh Gentle Reader, it came to pass that Jeff Brooks and Mike Redman shared a houseboat on Fairview, where they undertook to maintain some kind of a social life while enduring the financial and emotional stresses of slipping their then-current marital entanglements. That which follows is a legacy of that period, when dollars were tight but the social instincts were hyperactive.

It did not take us long to discover that it cost much less to double date and cook at home than it did to pay some establishment to do it for us. The booze seemed to be a bit less expensive also, and thus it came to pass that unused and highly rusted culinary skills were hit with the gastronomic equivalent of WD 40, cheap jug wine, and, so fortified, we got into social culinary survival.

Turkey was a natural for several reasons. It was cheap (still is), easy to do, tough to screw up, impressive, good, reasonably free of calories and, by reason of its role in the nation's holidays, evocative of good cheer. (It also takes quite a while to cook, and a shrewd host can take advantage of this to ply his guests with the nation's most popular drug during the interval to minimize criticism of his culinary effort when and if it finally appears.)

The oven on our houseboat, and perhaps yours, was NOT large enough to take an entire bird; but a half bird, in a roasting pan, did quite well. We were endowed with duplicate portions of the cooking ware and spices that had been part of our respective households. (You can imagine, dear friends, which halves of the couples had split with the pots, etc., but one of us had somehow escaped with a roasting pan.) We also had a 15-foot freezer which I'd lugged into freedom, and in that freezer we would keep turkey halves against the day of need.

One Thursday night Jeff informed me that he'd scored a deal that would keep us alive and socially active forever. Safeway had some humungous birds on sale at ridiculous prices and he'd scored two, neither of which took up less than two cubic feet apiece in the freezer. Upon questioning, he allowed as how he knew they wouldn't fit the oven in their present state but that he'd figured the solution was to take them to Pete's Midget Super and get Pete to run them through the saw. Under cross examination from his roommate, who enjoyed an occasional beer in the cooler with Pete, he allowed as how that might not be the best way to stay good buddies with the friendly neighborhood grocer.

There the matter, and the birds, rested for some months. Whatever the USDA guidelines may be for freezer life of turkeys, these birds were on their third lives when, one Saturday morning, we were flat up against it with dates that night, zero excess cash and nothing but the birds in the freezer. We rose, had coffee, discussed the problem and finally, Jeff resolved it with the suggestion that I use a circular saw while he showered, and then exited in that direction.

We had two circular saws, one each, since neither of our soon-to-be-ex's had had much interest in retaining one, and I chose his for the job. Removing the birds and putting them on our spotless counter in our spotless kitchen (Jeff, being a doc, was fanatic about cleanliness), I deftly identified and removed the plastic wrapping and the little wire device that kept the legs together and inserted Jeff's saw at the south end of the bird, pointing it in a northerly direction. It worked splendidly, despite the slippery, cold nature of the patient, but it became very clear that the saw's manufacturer hadn't contemplated this application.

You'll note, next time you see a circ saw in operation, that the sawdust which is generated in cutting is blown away by the wind the saw produces and, being blown to one side, drifts a bit and then settles. Not so, my friends, with the turkey dust. It stays together, wet and cohesive and is impelled in a straight line forward and up landing in neat lines on walls, countertops and the T-shirt worn by the operator. By the time Jeff emerged from the shower, two twenty-pound birds were in halves, five quarts of turkey dust had been applied to the walls, counters and saw. I passed him the latter while I headed for the shower, emerging to find the kitchen cleaned up, ditto the saw, and my roommate headed back to the shower for his second scrub of the day.

Turkey for Two, Four or More (FINALLY)

1/2 circ-saw turkey
1 roasting pan
1 bag stuffing mix (or stale bread torn up
    and spiced with whatever's leafy and at hand)

Put turkey in pan over stuffing mix (follow mix directions) and cook at 359 F. until done. If you want gravy, chop the giblets and boil them in a pan for a bit. Add the chopped up liver and gizzard and the juices from the roasting pan. Add a little water or wine, if needed, then stir the liquid vigorously while adding flour to thicken. Piece of cake, eh? Oh...had five glasses of Chablis while you were waiting, did you? Pity...

Jeff Brooks and Mike Redman

ROSEMARY CITRUS CHICKEN

4 boneless chicken breasts
1 cup red wine
1/2 cup orange juice
1/4 cup lime juice
1/8 cup lemon juice
1 T. crushed rosemary

Serves 2.

Mix wine, juices and rosemary. Pour over chicken and marinate in refrigerator for 4-6 hours or all day. Bake covered at 425 F. for 45 minutes, or grill chicken on barbecue, basting with marinade while cooking.

Sheri Gotay

*F*reshly squeezed juices and a few sprigs of fresh rosemary make this dish really tasty!

GREEK CHICKEN IN PHYLLO

1 cup almonds, toasted for 10-15 minutes at 350 F. and
    coarsely chopped
3 cups cooked chicken, chopped into bite-size pieces
8 oz. feta cheese, crumbled
1/2 cup sliced green onion
3/4 cup cream
2 T. Dijon mustard
1/2 tsp. basil
1 clove garlic, minced
1 tsp. herb pepper
1/2 lb. phyllo dough
Melted butter

Serves 4-6.

Mix together all ingredients except phyllo dough and butter.

Divide phyllo dough in half. Brush each sheet with a little butter and layer one half of the dough into a lasagne-type baking dish.

Add chicken mixture. Cover with the remaining phyllo dough one sheet at a time, brushing each sheet with butter. With a sharp knife, cut a couple of slits in the top and pop it into the oven. Bake at 375 F. for 30 minutes.

Kirvil Skinnerland

One year a duck made her nest 3 feet outside our kitchen window. After several weeks we felt bonded by observing her while washing dishes. It was a shock to look out one morning and see her gone, the nest destroyed, eggshells strewn about. Raccoons must have struck in the night. As I studied the situation, Mama Duck returned. She studied the situation and turned toward me and let out an accusing string of quacks. "I didn't do it," I pleaded. She flew away and never returned.

Ann Bassetti

RAFTING UP

Pastas, Casseroles and Side Dishes

MANICOTTI WITH TOMATO SAUCE

*P*eople often ask if it's safe to swim in Lake Union. As one of the few deep fresh water ports on the West Coast, Lake Union has long been used for industrial purposes. Unfortunately this use left the lake with very polluted sediments. The water, however, is quite clean. All houseboats have been hooked up to the city sewers for about 25 years.

The main pollution comes from storm sewer overflow. The city is actively trying to resolve that problem, as well as to encourage recreational boaters to empty their tanks at an appropriate dump site.

Many houseboaters consider it a great pleasure to come home, hot and tired, and dive off the deck! As long as it's not after a big storm, and we don't muck around in the sediments, we feel quite safe enjoying the water.

Houseboat Old-timer

Stuffing:
1/2 lb. ground beef
1 clove garlic, minced
1/4 cup olive oil
1 cup ricotta cheese
4 ounces mozzarella cheese, grated
1 egg lightly beaten
1/2 tsp. salt
1/2 tsp. dried oregano

Tomato Sauce:
1/2 cup chopped onions
1/2 cup chopped green peppers
2 cloves garlic, minced
1/2 cup olive oil
1 2-pound can whole tomatoes
1 cup tomato purée
1 tsp. salt
1 tsp. sugar
1/2 tsp. dried oregano, crumbled
1/2 tsp. dried basil, crumbled
1/2 pound mushrooms, sliced

8 manicotti
Freshly ground Parmesan cheese

Serves 4

Stuffing: Brown beef and garlic in olive oil. Drain off any fat and place the beef and garlic in a bowl. Stir in ricotta and mozzarella cheeses, beaten egg, salt and oregano. Set aside.

Tomato Sauce: Sauté onions, green peppers and garlic in olive oil until onions are transparent. Add remaining ingredients, mix well and simmer for at least 1 hour — the longer the better. Adjust seasonings.

Preheat oven to 350 F. Cook manicotti in boiling salted water for 8 to 10 minutes or until *al dente*. Drain them and allow to cool. Fill them with stuffing and place in a buttered shallow baking dish. Cover with sauce. Sprinkle generously with Parmesan cheese, cover with foil, bake for 15 minutes. Remove foil and bake for another 10 minutes until heated through and bubbly.
Theresa Harvey

PASTA À LA PUTANESCA

1/3 cup olive oil
9 anchovies
8 whole peeled garlic cloves
1/4 tsp. dried red pepper flakes
1 28 oz. can tomatoes, chopped (or 4 ripe tomatoes chopped)
2 tsp. capers
12 Calamata olives, pitted & halved
5 garlic cloves chopped
1/3 cup chopped fresh parsley
1 T. chopped fresh basil
3/4 lb. pasta
Extra chopped parsley for garnish

Serves 4.

Heat oil in skillet. Add the anchovies and whole garlic. Cook until garlic cloves brown and anchovies fall apart. Add red pepper and cook a few seconds more.

Add tomatoes, olives & capers. Simmer sauce for 30 minutes. Add the chopped garlic, parsley and basil to the sauce and simmer a bit longer.

Cook pasta, toss with 1/2 the sauce until well coated. Arrange pasta on platter and pour remaining sauce on top. Sprinkle chopped parsley all over and serve.

Michael McCrackin

This sauce can be doubled or tripled. It is wonderful to make in advance and freeze. Come home from work, thaw it out, cook pasta, and dinner is ready! Accompany with green salad, red wine and French bread.

ROYAL FLUSH PASTA

This is a simple but extremely delicious pasta. It's an absolute must to use fresh mozzarella. You can vary the amount of the other ingredients depending on how many people you are serving or how hungry you are. Good olive oil and fresh basil are important too.

3-4 large ripe tomatoes,chopped
1/4 cup chopped fresh basil
1/3 cup good olive oil
1/2 cup fresh mozzarella, sliced or cubed
Crushed garlic to taste
Salt and pepper to taste
1 lb. pasta (fusilli, mostaccioli or pastas that hold sauce well)
Fresh grated Parmesan cheese

Serves 2-4.

Combine tomatoes, basil, olive oil, mozzarella, garlic, salt and pepper in medium bowl and let marinate for at least one hour at room temperature. Cook and drain pasta and toss with marinade. Serve immediately. Sprinkle with fresh grated Parmesan.

Lani Stone from Ladies Poker Night

LIBERATED SPAGHETTI SAUCE

8 oz. lean ground beef
1 medium onion
1/2 tsp. garlic powder
Salt and pepper
1 12-oz. can tomato paste
1 15-oz. can tomato sauce
1 15-oz. can stewed tomatoes
1 1/2 cups chopped fresh mushrooms
1 tsp. oregano
1 tsp. basil
2 bay leaves
3 T. Worcestershire sauce
Dash Tabasco sauce

Serves 6.

Brown ground beef with chopped onion, salt, pepper, and garlic. Drain and combine with remaining ingredients. Simmer over low heat for an hour or until sauce is reduced. Stir frequently. Serve over pasta of your choice.

Bill Keasler
(President of the Floating Homes Association since 1980)

This recipe was born in my desperate days following a feminist epiphany early in our marriage. We had suddenly decided that I would henceforth be responsible for the kitchen every other week. Although most of what I invented then is best forgotten, this stuff endures because it reheats well and everybody seems to like it.

MARIE'S PORK-OUT LASAGNA

Lasagna without pork chops is no longer lasagna around our houseboat since I discovered this wonderful recipe.

1 lb. ground beef
2 lean pork chops, cut up
1 medium onion
Garlic and celery to taste
1 15 oz. can tomatoes
1 small can tomato paste
Salt, pepper and oregano to taste
1 lb. cottage cheese
1/2 lb. jack cheese, shredded
1/2 lb. mozzarella cheese, shredded
Lasagna noodles (small package)
1 cup Parmesan cheese

Serves several "Garfields" or 6-8 people.

Simmer first seven ingredients until cooked down and thick. In a 9" x 13" baking dish, layer cooked and drained noodles, meat sauce and cheeses until all is used. Cover with Parmesan. Bake at 350 F. until cheese is melted.

Marie Johnston

ASPARAGUS LASAGNA

Several bunches of medium size asparagus*
1 1/2 qts. half & half
1 qt. whole milk
1/4 lb. butter
8 T. olive oil
1 cup flour
1 tsp. nutmeg
2 T. mixed dried Italian herbs
Salt to taste
1 1/2 lbs. mozzarella cheese sliced very thin (have deli slice it)
2 cups parmesan cheese, shredded
1 cup fresh herbs (rosemary, parsley, basil snipped or chopped finely)**
3/4 lb. lasagna noodles

Serves 8-10.

Cook lasagna *al dente* and drain. Break off and discard stems and wash asparagus; slice on the diagonal into 1 inch pieces. Lightly steam, drain and rinse with cold water so it retains its green color.

Melt butter in large sauce pan. Add oil. Add flour and stir with a whisk until smooth. Gradually add the milk and cream and keep stirring until smooth and thick (but do not boil).

Butter a 9" x 13" baking dish (there will be enough for a small pan also). Layer sauce, noodles, sauce, asparagus, herbs, sauce, mozzarella, parmesan, sauce, noodles, sauce, mozzarella, parmesan. Bake at 325 F. covered until bubbly. Remove cover and cook about 10 more minutes to lightly brown the top.

Jann McFarland

*The amount of asparagus doesn't really matter — I use as much as I can afford! If you use large, fat asparagus, most of it will be tossed out, so medium size is best.

**If you use dried herbs, substitute 1 tsp. each of thyme, parsley and rosemary. Dried basil doesn't do much.

The first time we took our cat to a land house to visit he wouldn't step off the patio onto the grass. He apparently thought it was water. Finally he tentatively put a paw out and then waited for it to sink. When it didn't, he walked across the lawn with great deliberation, holding his paws up high.

This recipe came out of a magazine some years back. It sat unused, like most recipes I clip, until my husband Clay discovered it. It has now become his specialty and has been carried out to a few Pig Roast tables, family gatherings, and sometimes we even have it at home. It's good the next day, too.

SECOND-HAND SPINACH LASAGNA

1 lb. ricotta cheese
1 1/2 cups shredded mozzarella cheese
1 egg
1 pkg. (10 oz.) frozen chopped spinach (thawed and drained)
1 tsp. salt
3/4 tsp. oregano
1/8 tsp. pepper
2 jars (15.5 oz. each) spaghetti sauce
1/2 pkg. lasagna noodles (8 oz.), uncooked
1 cup water

Serves 8.

Mix ricotta, 1 cup of the mozzarella, egg, spinach, salt, oregano and pepper. In a greased 13" x 9" x 3" baking dish, layer 1/2 cup spaghetti sauce, 1/3 of the noodles and half of the cheese mixture. Repeat. Top with rest of noodles, then remaining sauce. Sprinkle with rest of Mozzarella. Pour water around the edges. Cover tightly with foil. Bake at 350 F. for one hour and 15 minutes or until bubbly. Let stand for 15 minutes or so before serving.

Kris Eaton

PASTA OVERBOARD

2 cups sun dried tomatoes in oil (including oil), slivered
6 cloves garlic, minced or grated
16 oz. brie cheese, rind removed (room temperature)
3/4 cup kalamata olives, pitted and sliced
2 cups fresh basil, chopped (measure before chopping and do
    not pack)
1 cup toasted pine nuts
Parmesan cheese
2 lbs. pasta

Serves 6-8.

In a large bowl, use a potato masher to "moosh" brie cheese, oil and
tomatoes, olives, garlic and basil together. Cook pasta *al dente*. Drain
and toss with sauce. Add pine nuts, toss again and serve with Parmesan
cheese sprinkled on top.

Jann and Sid McFarland

Houseboats are appealing locations for celebrations. We were married on a raft outside our first small houseboat. A small family contingent joined us, taking turns keeping the toddler out of the water. Our neighbors held their own party to cheer us on and the ducks ate the confetti! Another couple had their wedding reception on the dock, complete with a band. The only crisis was when all 100 plus guests went to the end of the dock — at the same time — to witness the arrival of the bride and groom by motor launch and almost sank the dock!

Ann Bassetti

PASTA WITH SUN-DRIED TOMATOES, OLIVES AND GOAT CHEESE

2 large garlic cloves, minced
3/4 cup finely chopped onion
2 T. olive oil
2/3 cup sun dried tomatoes (oil packed), drained
1/2 cup chicken broth
1/4 cup kalamata (brine cured) olives, pitted and sliced
1/3 cup chopped fresh parsley
1/2 lb. medium-size pasta shells
1 cup crumbled mild goat cheese (such as Montrachet)
Additional goat cheese to sprinkle on top of pasta

Serves 2.

Sauté garlic and onion in olive oil over low heat, stirring, until onion is soft. Add tomatoes and broth and simmer until liquid is reduced by one third. Stir in olives, parsley and salt and pepper to taste and keep mixture warm. Cook pasta in kettle of boiling salted water until *al dente* and drain, reserving 1/3 cup of the cooking water. In a serving bowl, whisk 3 oz. of the goat cheese with the hot water until melted and smooth. Add pasta and tomato mixture and toss well. Sprinkle with extra goat cheese.

Mary Gey-McCulloch and Fred McCulloch

ORECCHIETTE WITH SPINACH AND GARLIC

2 bunches (about 12 oz. each) spinach, rinsed well and drained
12 oz. dry orecchiette (cup-shaped) or ruote (wheel-shaped)
    pasta
1/3 cup olive oil
6 cloves garlic, minced or pressed
1/2 tsp. crushed dried hot red chiles
Salt
1/3 to 1/2 cup Parmesan cheese

Makes 6 first course servings.

Remove and discard spinach stems; chop leaves coarsely and set aside.
In a 6 or 8 quart pan, cook orecchiette in 4 quarts boiling water just until tender to bite (12 to 15 minutes); or cook according to package directions. Just before pasta is done, stir in spinach. Cook, uncovered, stirring to distribute spinach, just until water returns to a full boil. Drain
pasta and spinach.

While pasta is cooking, heat oil in a wide frying pan over medium heat.
Stir in garlic and chiles. Cook, uncovered, until garlic turns opaque
(about 2 minutes). Add pasta and spinach to pan; mix lightly, using 2
spoons. Season to taste with salt. Serve with the Parmesan cheese.

Brigitte Erickson

We houseboaters have our own "time capsule" which can be opened centuries from now to reveal our history. That capsule is the bottom of the lake. There is not a single houseboater who doesn't have a story about something they've dropped in the lake. We all know that if a project requires 10 nails, you must buy 2 extra to sacrifice to the lake. Right off my front deck, about 40 feet down, there are at least these items: a $300 pager, 2 pairs of Oakley sunglasses, a hammer, an assortment of coffee cups, wine glasses and snack plates, and a winch handle from our sailboat. The muck at the bottom is so deep that divers don't have much luck retrieving small items.

Houseboat Old-timer

PASTA WITH SMOKED MUSSELS AND HORSERADISH

1 cup sour cream
1/2 cup cream
1/2 cup grated fresh horseradish
3 T. red wine vinegar
1 T. Dijon mustard
1 tsp. sugar
Salt and pepper to taste
1 lb. pasta, cooked and drained
1 onion, grated or chopped fine
2 3 1/2 oz. cans smoked mussels
3 T. chives

Serves 4.

In food processor or blender, blend sour cream, cream, horseradish, vinegar, mustard, sugar, salt and pepper to taste. In a large bowl, stir together the sauce, onion, cooked pasta, mussels, and toss until well mixed. Garnish with chives. Serve either hot or at room temperature.

Bruce Knott

PASTA WITH GARLIC, ANCHOVIES, AND CHAMPIGNONS

Olive oil
Flat fillets of anchovies (how many per person depends on
how much you like anchovies — I use 5 or 6, but then
   I like 'em)
A few cloves of garlic, sliced fine (again, depends on taste
   — I use one clove per person)
A few flakes of hot red pepper (how much depends on
   you-know-what)
6 medium-sized or 9 small mushrooms per person
1/2 lb. of fresh spaghettini for every 2 people

Servings depend on quantities used.

Put water for pasta on to boil. Start the pasta when the water is ready.

Heat the olive oil in a small pot (enough to cover the bottom of the pot
well) and fry the garlic slices very gently until they begin to turn gold.

Add the anchovies, mashing them into the oil and garlic with a wooden
spoon, until what you have is basically a runny paste.

Add the pepper flakes, mix again, then throw in the mushrooms. Toss
until each mushroom is lightly covered in the sauce. (You're on very
low heat all the time.) Remove from the heat. (You don't cook the
mushrooms through, just enough to braise them.)

Take out the mushrooms, and toss the pasta (which has meanwhile
cooked to *al dente* perfection) in the oil-garlic-anchovy mix. (I'd say
"sauce", but it's not really runny enough to be a sauce.)

Top with the mushrooms and serve with a green salad.

Lesley Hazleton

*T*his is quick, simple and good!

Leonard and Marie Johnston were home during both the 1964 Alaska earthquake and the local big one in 1965. In both cases they report it felt as if their houseboat dropped straight down about 1 foot.

At an early hour one day in 1992, many houseboaters were awakened by their houses lurching wildly. Because of the odd hour someone made the connection with the day's major headline and called the U of W geology department. Yes, they confirmed, tremors do travel such great distances and are more readily felt in the water — we had been "hit" by the Los Angeles earthquake!

CLAM LINGUINI

1/2 cup olive oil
1 large onion, chopped
3 large cloves garlic, minced
1/2 cup fresh minced basil
1 T. oregano
Salt and pepper to taste
1 cup fresh minced parsley
2 cans clams, including liquid
2 T. Romano or Parmesan cheese, grated
1 lb. spaghetti or linguini, cooked *al dente*

Serves 3-4.

Combine first 7 ingredients and cook until thickened, about 15 minutes. Add clams to warm. Toss with pasta and top with grated cheese.

Dawn Vyvyan

PAELLA

6 chicken breasts
2 12 oz. cans chicken broth
1 4 oz. jar pimientos
1 clove garlic, minced
1 medium onion, minced
1 stalk celery, chopped
1/2 lime, juiced
1 can baby clams, drained
1 can shrimp, drained
1 1/2 cups converted rice
1 10.5 oz. pkg. frozen peas
5 T. olive oil
1/4 tsp. saffron
1/3 cup flour
1/2 tsp. salt
1/8 tsp. pepper
Fresh crab, optional

Serves 4-6.

Bone chicken and remove skin and cut in 3/4" strips. Mix flour, salt and pepper in plastic bag. Add chicken to bag and shake well to coat chicken. Remove chicken and shake off excess flour. Heat 3 T. oil in pan and sauté chicken on medium or low heat until light brown, turning frequently. Cut pimientos in half lengthwise and then in 1/4" strips. Set aside chicken and pimientos.

In a deep pot heat 2 T. oil and add rice. Cook over low heat, stirring constantly, until rice turns deep yellow. Add onion, garlic and celery and sauté 1 minute longer. Add chicken broth, saffron and lime juice and bring to a boil slowly. Add chicken, pimientos, clams, shrimp and stir well. Reduce heat to low and cook covered for about 20 minutes. Cook peas separately and add to mixture. For an extra touch, add fresh crab just before serving.

Raquel Johnston

*I*t is well known that cats like to bring "offerings" to their owners. Houseboat cats follow the tradition, bringing crawdads and small fish!

2025 CHICKEN DIVAN

2 bunches broccoli, cut in medium pieces
3 chicken breasts
2 cans cheddar cheese soup
1 cup mayonnaise
Juice of 1/2 lemon
2 T. curry powder or to taste
1 lb. cheddar cheese, grated
2 cans French fried onion rings

So many houseboaters have become "Chicken Divan" addicts that it always shows up at dock potlucks.

Serves 6.

Cook, bone and shred chicken into bite size pieces. Steam broccoli until barely tender, drain, and arrange in greased 9" x 13" baking dish. Arrange chicken on top of broccoli. Combine soup, mayonnaise, lemon juice and curry powder and pour over chicken. Spread cheese over top. Cover with foil and bake at 350 F. until bubbly. Remove foil. Sprinkle onion rings over top and cook 10 more minutes to lightly brown.

Judy Barnes

OVERNIGHT CHICKEN RICE CASSEROLE

1 box long grain and wild rice mix
4 large chicken breasts
1 cup celery leaves and tops, chopped
1 tsp. onion powder
1 tsp. marjoram
1 tsp. fines herbes
1 cup chopped celery
1 medium onion, chopped
1 medium green bell pepper, chopped
2 4 oz. cans water chestnuts, drained and chopped
2 cans cream of chicken soup
3/4 cup mayonnaise
3/4 cup buttered bread crumbs

Serves 12.

Prepare rice as directed on package.

Cook chicken in salted water to cover, seasoned with celery leaves and tops, onion powder, marjoram and fines herbes. When chicken is tender, remove from bones and dice.

Combine remaining ingredients except bread crumbs with chicken and rice and mix well. Put into buttered 9" x 12" casserole. Sprinkle top with buttered bread crumbs. Let stand in refrigerator overnight.

Bake at 325 F. for 1 hour.

Sharon Evered

First Meal of the Day

Yawn!

Meoww, meoww, meoww.

Shuffle shuffle down the stairs.

Light on — meoww.

Pick up cat dish, put on counter —

meoww, meowwwww.

Open drawer, grab can opener —

meoww, meoww, meoww.

Open cupboard, grab cat food —

meoww, meoww, meoww.

Put 3 scoops of dry cat food in

bowl — meowwww.

Open canned cat food, put in bowl,

break into bite-sized pieces —

meow, meow, meow.

Put bowl under steps.

Purrrr!

Crunch, crunch.

Shuffle upstairs to shower and start

the day.

West the Cat

Hazel Nigh, the "Queen Mother" of the Log Foundation moorage cooperative, recently celebrated her 85th birthday at a party given by her neighbors and friends in front of her houseboat. Hazel bought her first houseboat in 1948 for $2100. The seller, however, had neglected to tell her that her moorage, by the old steam plant at the south end of the Lake Union, was terminated and there was no place to tie up her houseboat. (Many houseboats from those moorages were warehoused at the south end of the lake.) Hazel then found moorage at Cadranell's Landing where she moored for three years. But her house crossed Lake Union twice more before she finally settled at 2019 Fairview in 1955. Since that time her beautiful flowers (not to mention her longevity!) have been an inspiration to all her neighbors.

Art Hemenway

NOODLE BAKE

1 1/2 lbs. ground beef
2 T. butter
1 tsp. salt
Dash pepper
1 T. sugar
2 8 oz. cans tomato sauce
1 8 oz. pkg. noodles, cooked and drained
2 cloves garlic
6 green onions, chopped, including tops
1 pint sour cream
2 cups grated cheddar cheese
1 3 oz. pkg. cream cheese

Serves 6.

Melt butter in skillet, add ground beef and cook until brown. Crush garlic fine and mix with salt, pepper, sugar and tomato sauce. Add tomato mixture to the ground beef. Cover and simmer for 15 minutes. Mix green onions with cream cheese and sour cream in a large bowl, add noodles and toss. Grease 9" x 13" baking dish and put layer of noodle mixture in bottom, then a layer of meat and tomato sauce. Repeat until all is used, ending with meat and tomato. Spread grated cheese over the top and bake at 350 F. for 30 minutes or until bubbly.

Hazel Nigh

Floating Homes Association

VEGETARIAN SHEPHERD'S PIE

1 T. olive oil
2 carrots, chopped in bite size pieces
1 onion, chopped in bite size pieces
1 clove garlic, pressed
1 red bell pepper, chopped in bite size pieces
1 zucchini, chopped in bite size pieces
8 to 12 mushrooms, sliced
1 14.5 oz. can chopped, peeled tomatoes
1 1/2 tsp. oregano
1 1/2 tsp. basil
1 tsp. salt
5-6 potatoes, preferably Yellow Finns
1-2 T. butter (or garlic butter)
1/3 cup milk
Grated Parmesan or cheddar cheese for garnish
Paprika for garnish

Serves 3-4.

Sauté carrots, onion and garlic in olive oil for 5 minutes. Add red pepper, zucchini and mushrooms and sauté another 5 minutes, or until all vegetables are starting to soften. Add tomatoes, oregano, basil and salt to skillet and sauté until vegetables are desired texture, about 5 more minutes.

Clean and cube potatoes and cook in salted water until soft, about 15 minutes. Drain, and mash. Add butter or garlic butter and milk and stir until blended. Potatoes are mashed, but some texture is maintained by skins and perhaps a few lumps. Add salt to taste.

Put vegetable mixture in a square 8" Pyrex or metal pan. Top with mashed potatoes. Garnish with Parmesan or cheddar and paprika. Put under broiler just long enough to brown lightly, about 5 minutes.

Caroline Cropp

This dish is also good served in individual casseroles. And it's a great potluck dish. It's nutritious, high in beta carotenes, low in fat, and easy on the Earth.

*T*his is not a quick and easy recipe. It takes time, a bit of dedication, and a willingness to "work" with what you are preparing — like cooking in the old days. "Pyrohy", along with "Sour Mushroom Soup" and "Sweet Dough Yeast Bread" (see recipes) are part of my family's traditional Christmas Eve Ukrainian-Polish dinner. I'm sorry that I don't have the traditional names for any but the Pyrohy.

PYROHY ("UKRAINIAN RAVIOLI")

Dough:
5 cups all purpose flour
1 tsp. salt
2 T. oil
3 eggs, beaten
3/4 cup cold water ("more or less," my mother says!)

Potato-cheese filling:
6 lbs. potatoes, cooked, drained and mashed
1/2 lb. cheddar cheese, grated or cut into small chunks
Salt and pepper to taste
1 medium onion, chopped fine
1/4 lb. butter or margarine

Sauerkraut filling:
1 large can sauerkraut, drained*
1 small onion, diced
1/4-1/2 cup water

Lekvor filling:
1 jar lekvor (prune jelly available at most large grocery stores)

Saude:
2 onions, chopped and sautéed in butter or margarine

Serves 8.

Dough: In a deep bowl mix the flour with salt and add oil, eggs and enough water to make a medium-soft dough. Knead on a floured board or countertop until smooth (too much kneading will make the dough tough). Return dough to bowl, cover and refrigerate for 30 minutes. The dough can be filled with 3 different fillings.

Potato-cheese filling: Brown onion in butter. Mix all ingredients together and set aside.

Sauerkraut filling: Mix all ingredients in pot and stew for about 20 minutes or until very limp and no longer crunchy.

Lekvor filling: Use straight from the jar.

Assembly: Take dough from refrigerator. Cut off a piece about the size of a large orange. Roll dough on well-floured surface until 1/16" thick or a little thinner than a pie crust. Cut the dough sheet into 3 1/2 inch squares. Put 1-1 1/2 heaping teaspoons of a filling in the center of each square. Fold the dough over on itself and using your fingers (sometimes you need to wet them a bit) press the edges securely closed. Put aside on a dry towel and continue the process until the dough is used up. Boil water in a large pot (Mom used a roasting pan). Add a little salt and oil. Drop the pyrohys into the water individually and cook about 5 minutes or until done. Drain.

While they are boiling, sauté 2 onions in butter or margarine until brown. Pour over cooked pyrohys.

*Save the juice for Sour Mushroom Soup (see recipe) or drink it for your health!

Susan Chatlos-Susor

DEPRESSION CASSEROLE

This recipe got its name when our dock sponsored a Hillbilly Party with a Lake Union skydiving exhibition. It was a blistering hot day, and we had boats sprinkled around the Lake to collect people and parachutes from the water, a slushy machine putting out peach daiquiris, and a band playing rowdy music. Some of us were a little surprised to suddenly see the skydivers streak, literally, into the water, wearing parachutes but nothing else. This dish is named for the al fresco parachutist who made a BIG impression and a little depression when she missed the water and landed in the midst of the crowd on the dock.

1 lb. bacon, snipped into pieces
1 onion, chopped
1-2 lbs. extra lean ground meat
1 T. chili powder
1 tsp. salt
Pepper
1 large can whole tomatoes
1 large can tomato paste
1 medium can stewed tomatoes
1 pkg. egg noodles
2 T. butter
1 lb. fresh mushrooms, sliced
1 1/2 cups cheddar cheese, grated
1 1/2 cups mozzarella cheese, grated

Serves a crowd.

Cook bacon pieces until crisp. Remove and drain on a paper towel. In the bacon fat, sauté onion. Remove the onion and drain. Pour all bacon fat from pan.

In same pan add ground meat and brown. Add at least 1 T. chili powder, 1 tsp. salt, and coarse ground pepper to taste. (Do not add too much salt at this point, you can correct the amount later.) Add whole tomatoes, tomato paste and stewed tomatoes. Return the bacon and onions to the mixture. Simmer for at least 1/2 hour.

Add butter to boiling salted water and cook egg noodles until tender but firm. Combine the drained noodles and the tomato-meat mixture in a large bowl. Add the mushrooms.

Put mixture in buttered casserole dishes (it is a large amount). Top with grated cheeses.

Before serving, pop into a 350 F. oven for about half an hour to melt the cheese and blend the flavors. I usually make this up a day ahead of time, so I can enjoy the party (and the view).

Shirley Thomas

ANNIE'S GOOP IN A POT

1 lb. sausage
1 lb. ground beef
1 large can mushrooms
1 large can tomatoes
1 large can kidney beans
1 T. chili powder
1 large onion, chopped
1 green pepper, chopped
1 stalk celery, chopped
1 T. or more parsley
8 oz. pasta (shell or elbow macaroni)

Serves 6.

Brown sausage and ground beef with salt and pepper to taste. While browning, add onion, celery, green pepper and parsley. De-grease when done.

In large pot add rest of ingredients, including juices from canned beans and tomatoes. Simmer 10-15 minutes

Add pasta and cook until pasta is done.

Michael McCrackin

This is a family recipe by our Italian Auntie in Omak. It can be easily doubled or tripled for large crowds. Very popular on picnics and outings, especially summer houseboat parties.

WILD CHILES RELLENOS

8 green chiles, roasted and peeled*
1 cup Jack cheese, cubed
2 eggs
About 1/2 cup flour
1/2 tsp. salt (not necessary)
Cooking oil

Serves 4

*Put on rubber gloves. Slit the pods lengthwise and remove seeds and veins. Place pods on a cookie sheet under broiler (or on your outdoor grill). Allow pods to blister well on each side. Turn frequently so they don't burn. Remove from fire and cover with damp towels for 15 minutes. Peel skin from stem downward. Chiles are now ready to use (or to freeze if you're tired). [OR: Take whole chiles and blister with propane torch in the sink (much faster). Peel and slice just enough to remove seeds and insert filling. Editor.]

If you don't have time for the above, go to the grocery and buy a can of Ortego whole roasted green chiles.

Separate egg whites and yolks. Beat whites until stiff. Mix flour and salt with yolks until smooth but not too thick. Fold yolk and flour mixture into beaten whites.

Fill each chile with cheese. Lightly flour chiles so batter will stick. Dip into beaten eggs for a liberal coating. Fry in moderately hot oil until golden brown. Serve with Spanish rice and beans or posole and some red chile sauce.

Ron Steward

First you must go to New Mexico and catch your green chiles. The best places to find them are in the Mesilla and Espanola valleys or the Chimayo area. Select full-bodied, firm, straight chiles, allowing 2 per person. Bring them home for roasting. If you like this dish, go back to New Mexico and bring home some red chiles too, and make the sauce. You'll like it even more.

MUDDY TACOS

1 onion, diced
2 T. canola oil
3-4 cups (or two 16 oz. cans) black beans, cooked
    (kidney or pinto beans will do in a pinch. I cook beans
    ahead and freeze them)
1 large bell pepper, diced (any color — I prefer red)
1-2 tomatoes, diced
5-6 green onions, diced
1-2 cups lettuce, shredded

Dressing:
2-3 T. olive or canola oil
1/4 cup red wine vinegar
1 large clove garlic, minced or pressed
1/2 tsp. ground cumin
Salt & pepper to taste

12 large flour or whole wheat tortillas
Nonfat yogurt
1 1/2 cups cheddar cheese, shredded

Serves 6.

Sauté onions about 5 minutes until clear. Add beans, stir and heat through.

In a bowl mix the dressing ingredients, then add the bell pepper, tomatoes, green onions and lettuce and toss.

Wrap the tortillas in tin foil and heat in 250 F. oven. (Do not nuke tortillas in the microwave except in emergency -- makes them tough.)

Assemble the tacos by laying a glob of beans down the middle of the tortilla, the "salad mixture" on top of that, and a little nonfat yogurt and/or some shredded cheddar cheese on top of that. Roll 'em up. (Or better yet, tell the troops to assemble their own while you go take a long, hot bath!)

Beth Means

I keep the ingredients for this popular dinner around the house at all times for those evenings when we come home tired, cold, and muddy or when I'm just not in the mood for cooking. Yummy, filling, reasonably cheap, and very easy.

This recipe fermented in 1978 on seeing how fecund was the landfill that created the mound at Gasworks Park. Independent of the hulks or antediluvian intestine-like maze of lurking cracking towers, the mound took on a life of its own. The soil soon grew all kinds of unplanned wonders — potatoes, tomatoes and other interesting, though illegal herbs. "This must be memorialized," I thought. "What can remind us of these inner workings; of petrol, emerging plant life and malodorous fecal soil that could give someone else a taste of and an enduring recollection of this process; of the earth's digestive processes, the reductional flatulence that is so naturally produced here?" What it must be is a little bitter, a little sweet, a little hot (or maybe a lot), a little legume and protein and veggies brewed in a steaming pot — and don't forget the herbs. Hence, Gasworks Chili!

GASWORKS CHILI

2 cups kidney beans
1 quart water
3/4 cup chopped onions
2 garlic cloves, minced
1/2 cup vegetable oil
1 lb. lean ground beef
1 tsp. fines herbes
2 tsp. salt
1/2 quart hot giardiniera vegetables
1/2 cup chopped green bell peppers
1 can tomato puree
1 to 3 tsp. chili powder
2 tsp. chile pepper seeds (to taste)
2 tsp. fresh oregano

Serves 6.

Fly a kite to test the winds.

Soak beans overnight in water with half amount of oil. Bring slowly to boil in same water, adding more if necessary, OR...

Bring water to a rolling boil. Add half amount of oil and salt. Add beans without stopping boiling. Reduce heat and simmer 2 to 2 1/2 hours.

Sauté meat, garlic and onions in remaining oil, season with fines herbes and salt. Drain and dice giardiniera vegetables. Combine beans, meat and vegetables in pot. Add remaining ingredients, then remaining seasonings. Cook covered 30 to 45 minutes. Do not boil.

Serve over rice or with cheese.

T. G. Susor

EASY MEXICAN QUICHE

3/4 lb. chorizo sausage, casings removed
1/2 lb. ground beef
1 1/2 cups finely chopped onion
1 pkg. taco seasoning

1 16 oz. can refried beans
2 baked 9" deep dish pie crusts
1 4 oz. can diced mild green chiles, drained
2 cups shredded Monterey Jack cheese
2 cups shredded sharp cheddar cheese

8 eggs, beaten to blend
1 cup sour cream
1 cup guacamole
15 to 20 corn chips
1/2 cup shredded sharp cheddar cheese
Pitted black olives

Makes 2 quiches

Combine sausage, ground beef and onion in medium skillet over medium heat. Cook until onion is translucent and meats are cooked, about 12 minutes. Pour off fat. Add taco seasoning and mix well. Set aside.

Spread refried beans evenly over bottom of each crust. Sprinkle chiles over beans. Combine Jack and 2 cups of cheddar cheese. Sprinkle 1/2 cup over each crust. Divide sausage mixture between each, spreading evenly. Cover with remaining 3 cups mixed cheese, adding 1 1/2 cups to each. (Can be prepared 1 day ahead and refrigerated or 1 month ahead and frozen.)

Preheat oven to 350 F. Carefully pour half of beaten eggs into each quiche. Bake until toothpick inserted in centers comes out clean, about 30 minutes, covering edges of crust with foil if browning too quickly. Cool 10 minutes. Spread 1/2 cup sour cream evenly over top of each quiche. Spoon guacamole around inside edges of crusts. Stand corn chips in guacamole. Sprinkle 1/4 cup shredded cheddar cheese over top of each quiche. Garnish with olives and serve.

Becky Foley

Sometimes young beaver wander downstream from the Sammamish Slough into Lake Union looking for a tasty snack. The tender stems of the corkscrew willows which thrive on the logs under houseboats are a special delicacy. Ignorant of this, I planted a willow twig between some logs at the end of my raft. It was nearly six feet tall by late summer and gorgeous! One morning I awoke to a loud, sharp "fwap"! I jumped up in time to see a beaver towing some sticks toward shore. He'd eaten my willow for breakfast. I began to experiment with chickenwire. A fresh twig guarded by a free-standing wire fence lasted until mid-summer. The following year I built a two foot frame, wrapped it with chickenwire, and planted yet another twig inside. "Fwap!" I now have a four foot fence double wrapped with chickenwire. My willow is now 6 feet tall, and less gorgeous, but no "fwap!" yet.

Bill Keasler

CHOCOLATE CHILI

4 cups onion
1/2 cup olive oil
1 lb. ground pork
1 lb. ground beef
3 cups water
3 T. cumin
3 T. cocoa
1 1/2 tsp. cayenne
2 32 oz. cans beans
6 garlic cloves, chopped
4 cups tomato juice
5 T. chili powder
3 T. oregano
2 T. cinnamon
1 T. salt
2 or 3 T. corn meal

Serves 8-10

Brown meats and drain. Add all other ingredients, heat and serve.

Bruce Knott

TENAS CHUCK* CHILE RELLENOS

1 7 oz. can whole green chiles
1/2 lb. Jack cheese, cut into 3/4" by 3/4" by 4" strips
6 eggs, beaten with salt and pepper to taste
1 medium onion, minced
2 T. olive oil
4 cloves garlic, minced

Serves 6

In non-stick 9" omelet pan, heat olive oil and sauté minced onion and garlic over medium heat. Slit chiles and remove any seeds and charred skin. Wrap chiles around cheese strips and place star-fashion over sautéed onion and garlic. Beat eggs, salt and pepper together, then pour over chiles and cheese. Cover pan and let cook slowly on low heat until eggs are set (about 15 to 20 minutes). Turn out on hot plate and serve at once. Serve with a fruit salad.

Sally Hall

This recipe evolved after we enjoyed transplanted Mexican cookery in Arizona restaurants around Phoenix the year Joe and I went back to school there. It's an easy dish for boat suppers, too.

*"Tenas Chuck" is the name of a 2-dock houseboat moorage on the east side of Lake Union. The name is Chinook jargon for "Little Water", as opposed to "Hyas Chuck" which is the "Big Water" of Lake Washington.

WOK THE DOCK
BROCCOLI WITH BACON

*D*ucks and geese will walk right

into your house looking for a

handout. They are quite fond of

dry cat food. Just don't try to scare

them out the door — they panic and

make a terrible "mess"!

2 stalks broccoli, cut into 1/2" x 1/2" pieces
1/2 lb. bacon, cut into 1" x 1" pieces
1 can of sliced water chestnuts (optional)

Cooking sauce (optional):
1 T. cornstarch
1/4 tsp. sugar
1 T. dry sherry
2 T. oyster sauce
1/2 cup water or chicken broth
1 tsp. sesame oil

Fry bacon until cooked but still soft (not crisp). Drain and set aside.
Heat 2 T. vegetable oil. Add broccoli. Stir fry for approximately 30
seconds. Add 1/4 cup water. Cover and let steam for 2 minutes. Add
bacon and stir fry for another 30 seconds. Add optional cooking sauce
and cook, stirring until sauce bubbles and thickens.

Steve Hansen

CARROTS ÉTOUFFÉS

2 lbs. carrots, peeled and thinly sliced in rounds
1 medium onion, thinly sliced quarters
1 small green bell pepper, thinly-sliced lengths
1 cup sugar
3/4 cup white vinegar
1 cup tomato soup
1 tsp. Worcestershire sauce
1/2 cup salad oil
1 tsp. prepared mustard
Salt and pepper to taste

Cook carrots, drain, and cool. Layer with green pepper and onions. Combine remaining ingredients and heat. Pour this mixture over layered vegetables. Cover and refrigerate. Best when sets overnight or longer. Serve chilled.

Pam Hendrick Sanford

We haven't the foggiest idea what étouffés means, but we love the word. We once had to do battle for it in a hotly-contested Scrabble game that raged on the deck for several days.

Parsleyed Almond Rice

1/4 cup chopped almonds
1 cup long grain white rice
2 cups water
1/4 tsp. salt
4 T. unsalted butter
2 T. minced fresh parsley

Serves 4.

Preheat oven to 350 F. Spread almonds in shallow baking pan and toast in oven, shaking pan occasionally to prevent scorching, 5-6 minutes or until golden. Set aside to cool. Combine rice with water and salt in medium saucepan and bring to boil over medium-high heat. Cover pan, reduce heat to low, and simmer 25 minutes or until rice is tender. Cut butter into small pieces. Remove rice from heat. Add almonds, butter and parsley and toss with fork to combine. Serve with lamb kabobs (see "Raccoon Kabobs").

Becky Foley

SHELBY STREET BEANS

1 cup chopped onion
6 slices bacon, cut into 1/2" pieces
1 clove garlic
1/2 cup catsup
2 T. brown sugar
1 T. dry mustard
2 T. vinegar
2 cans pork and beans (1 16-oz. can and 1 31-oz. can)

Serves 6 bean freaks.

Sauté bacon, onion and garlic until brown. Add rest of ingredients and mix well. Bake 3 hours at 275 F., stirring occasionally.

Elaine Powell

Both this and the Blackberry Grunt recipe are part of the barbecue tradition on the Shelby Street moorage located on Portage Bay.

This is a tasty, robust dish, a meal in itself afloat or ashore, good for breakfast, lunch, and dinner anytime, but it should probably be avoided by excessively fastidious persons or those who ride in crowded elevators and lack self-confidence. A crew full of these frijoles can expect substantial advantage on the downwind leg of any Duck Dodge Boat Race, even to the extreme of other crews dousing their spinnakers to keep the Frijole boat well ahead.

HAMBURGER DAVE'S STRATEGIC FRIJOLES

1 lb. pinto beans
1/2 lb. salt pork (those who don't care for salt & grease
    should substitute bacon)
1 onion about the size of a tennis ball or
    substitute a tennis ball

Check the beans for pebbles or other foreign items. Soak the beans in water overnight. Chop up the salt pork and onion into very small pieces. Drain the beans. Replace the dirty water with fresh water to cover, add the salt pork and onions, and simmer the mix for an hour (we use a crock pot, but any covered cooking vessel will do). Then turn the heat down and let it all sit for a day or so, adding water from time to time as it evaporates. The frijoles are ready to eat anytime after the third or fourth hour, but they just keep getting better.

The recipe quantity fits a crock pot and will serve four or five hungry frijole lovers, or several times that many people who don't like them. The frijoles can be mashed up and reheated with a little butter, cooking oil, or bacon grease (preferred), to make Frijoles Refritos.

Dave Gardner

4TH OF JULY BAKED BEANS

1 any size can pork and beans
1 any size can (or greater) B & M Brick Oven Baked Beans
1 bell pepper, chopped
1 onion, chopped
1/3 cup catsup
2 T. prepared mustard
2 T. bacon grease or olive oil

Serves "any size".

In skillet sauté pepper and onions in oil or butter until onions are translucent. Dump into casserole dish and add all other ingredients. Mix well. Bake covered in microwave on high for 15 minutes or in oven (covered) at 400 F. until bubbly.

Jim Burks

This was always a hit at Jim's Famous Marathon 4th of July Party. He would put a raft across the channel between two docks, and he and his guests would set off all kinds of pyrotechnical wonders!

CALICO BEANS

1/2 lb. ground beef
1/2 lb. bacon
1 onion, chopped
1 28 oz. can baked beans
1 16 oz. can kidney beans, drained
1 16 oz. can lima beans, drained
1/2 cup catsup
3/4 cup brown sugar
2 T. vinegar
1 tsp. dry mustard

Serves 12.

Brown beef and bacon. Sauté onion; remove fat. Combine all ingredients in a heavy kettle and bake uncovered at 350 F. for 40 minutes.

Sharon Evered

EGGPLANT SANDWICH

2 medium eggplants
1 rustic Italian baguette
Olive oil
Sun-dried tomato spread (see recipe for Sun-dried
      Tomato Bruchetta)
3 balls fresh mozzarella
Parmesan cheese, grated
Black pepper
6 cloves garlic, pressed
Handful of fresh basil

Serves 4-6.

Slice eggplants into disks approximately 1/4 to 3/8 inch thick. Oil a heavy cookie sheet with olive oil and cover surface with layer of eggplant disks. Bake at 350 F. for 15 minutes (or until tender when pricked with a fork).

Slice baguette in half, lengthwise. Drizzle olive oil on both surfaces. When eggplant disks are ready, cover one of the baguette halves with a layer of disks. Spread over the eggplant a layer of sun-dried tomato spread.

Slice mozzarella into 1/2" thick slices and place on top of tomato layer. Then sprinkle with grated Parmesan cheese and fresh black pepper. Distribute squeezed garlic on top.

Distribute basil leaves on top of garlic. Then arrange a layer of eggplant and top with remaining baguette half. Wrap in foil and place in preheated oven at 375 F. for 20 minutes.

For smaller amounts, make individual sandwiches by slicing baguette into disks and assembling and wrapping individually in foil.

Blair Robbins and Bob Burk

Our kitchen is one of our favorite places. It is the oldest portion of our houseboat and the only area left virtually untouched during our major remodeling adventure. Originally, our home was an oyster barge and later it became living quarters that evolved and evolved. The kitchen is a remnant of the barge. To us, food is special, we enjoy selecting fresh produce at the Pike Place Market and take time to prepare and enjoy our meals.

EGGPLANT MOLD

*O*nce upon a time at a Floating Homes Association auction some folks bought a dinner for 8 people at my end-of-the-dock houseboat. We pulled this off in July — hot. The people paid so much for this dinner that I had to give them my very best. So I brought out my old Provincial Dinner recipes from the New York Times of long ago, and slaved for two days. It was all to be served at room temperature. With the superb Eggplant Mold came Boeuf en Daube and other precious items. Two friends helped me serve and pour the wine. We wore spotless white aprons. After cocktails on the deck and a performance by many Lake Union sailboats, the guests were seated. All was carefully served. One lady took a look at my gorgeous eggplant and screeched, "EEEuuuhh!! Slippery!" I never forgave her!

2 lbs. eggplant cut in 3/8" slices
2/3 cup olive oil
4 cups Italian plum tomatoes (or large can of same)
1 large clove garlic
1 medium onion chopped fine
1 "splat" of harissa*
1 cup plain yogurt
1/2 cup chicken stock
Salt & pepper to taste

Serves 8.

Salt the eggplant and set it aside for 30 minutes. Do not skin until later so it will hold its shape in the sauté. Rinse off salt with cold water; pat dry on towels.

Heat 2 T. of the olive oil in a large skillet until hazed. Add onion and sauté until light brown. Add plum tomatoes and garlic and cook, stirring occasionally until mixture is thick and pulpy. Add a little salt and pepper and a good splat of harissa. Total cooking time approximately 20-25 minutes. Set aside 1/3 of mixture for sauce.

Preheat oven to 350 F. Heat 2/3 cup less 2 T. olive oil in large skillet; brown eggplant gently. Then skin the slices.

Now, get out your Charlotte Russe mold (2 quarts). I told you this was fancy! I bought one specially for that party, but you can use any 2 quart mold to create this gorgeous thing. Place one big slice of eggplant in bottom of mold pan. Arrange in overlapping concentric circles, spreading each layer with some tomato mixture and dabs out of 1 cup of plain yogurt. End with eggplant. Cover with foil; bake until eggplant is very tender, about 40-50 minutes. LET COOL COMPLETELY IN MOLD.

Simmer remaining tomato mixture with 1/2 cup chicken stock in small saucepan until heated through, 2-3 minutes. Let cool to room temperature. To serve, unmold eggplant onto fancy platter; spoon sauce around base. Can prepare up to 24 hours ahead (sans sauce). Keep covered in refrigerator; bring to room temperature to serve.

*Harissa: Some don't know about this great snappy middle-eastern seasoning. It does wonders to zest up the tomato sauce.

Helen Mitchell

LOG FOUNDATION EGGPLANT CASSEROLE

1 eggplant, peeled and diced
5 slices bacon, diced
1 green bell pepper, chopped
1 large onion, chopped
1 large can tomatoes
1 T. brown sugar.
Cheddar or mozarella cheese, grated
Bread crumbs

Serves 2-4.

Preheat oven to 350 F.

Steam eggplant for 15 minutes.

Meanwhile, sauté bacon, green pepper, and onion. Add tomatoes and brown sugar. Cook on medium heat for 5 minutes.

Drain the eggplant and combine all the ingredients in a casserole dish. (I sometimes like to add 1 to 2 zucchini, fresh mushrooms, garlic, and/or fines herbes.) Top with a generous amount of grated cheese and bread crumbs. Bake for 30 minutes at 350 F.

Claire Tangvald

Many years ago my boyfriend got mad at me and snatched up my Sony Color TV and tossed it into the lake in 40 feet of water. He then clicked his heels together, saluted and came back inside where a friend and I were standing with our mouths gaping open. Being much too material minded, I (only) threatened to throw his fancy police scanner in also. So he grabbed it and stomped it to death to deprive me of the pleasure. Sixteen hours later a diver retrieved the TV. After emergency treatment with heat lamps and one new fuse, it worked fine and still does seventeen years later.

ZUCCHINI AND POTATO TIEN

2 or 3 medium zucchini, cut in thin slices
2 or 3 white new potatoes, sliced thin
8 cloves garlic, slivered
Olive oil (lots!)
Salt and pepper to taste
1 T. thyme leaves

Serves 4.

Try to find potatoes about the same diameter as the zucchini. Preheat oven to 400 F. Put enough olive oil in bottom of a 9" x 13" pan to coat. Alternate slices of zucchini and potatoes, overlapping in rows, usually about 4 rows going the long way in the pan. Sprinkle garlic slivers over vegetables. Paint a heavy coat of olive oil over top of vegetables. Add salt, pepper and thyme. Bake at least 1 hour. Vegetables will be brown and almost crisp. You can paint more oil on while vegetables are cooking — makes it even better. You can also mix in slices of Japanese eggplant or plum tomatoes for a variation. This goes well with barbecued meat or salmon.

Jann McFarland

CARROTS AND LENTILS

2 T. olive oil
2 carrots, sliced
1 cup dried lentils
1 tsp. marjoram
1 large onion, chopped
2 cloves garlic, minced
2 cups chicken broth
Salt and pepper to taste

Serves 4.

Sauté onion in oil about 8 minutes. Add carrots and garlic and heat 2
minutes more. Add lentils and broth, cover and simmer about 45
minutes, or until lentils are tender and broth is absorbed. Mix in
marjoram, salt and pepper and serve.

Bruce Knott

PONDICHERRY DAL WITH VEGETABLES

2 cups dried lentils (split yellow or green)
6 cups water
1/2 tsp. turmeric
1 tsp. salt
5 - 10 neem leaves or curry leaves (available at Indian
    food stores)
Any of onion, tomatoes, cilantro, cauliflower, green beans,
    carrots, potatoes, eggplant, chopped
2 T. chopped ginger
2 cloves garlic, pressed
1 small onion, diced
1 tsp. cumin seeds
2 T. ghee (clarified butter)
Cilantro for garnish
Lime juice for garnish

*T*his dish is nutritious, hearty and delicious on a cold, rainy night. The basic soup can be made ahead — it stays fresh in refrigerator up to a week.

Serves 4-5.

Cook lentils in water with turmeric, salt and neem or curry leaves for 1 hour; should be consistency of a hearty soup. Then add chopped vegetables of your choice. Cook about 20 minutes until a nice soft texture but not overcooked.

Sauté ginger, garlic, onion and cumin seeds in hot ghee until sizzling. Pour over individual bowls of soup. Then sprinkle with fresh chopped cilantro and lime juice. Serve immediately.

Caroline Cropp

AUNT EMMA'S CABBAGE

1 large head Savoy cabbage, cored
3 large cloves garlic, chopped
1 large potato, diced
1/2 cup olive oil
Salt to taste

Serves 4.

Boil the cabbage in salted water until barely tender. (The leaves will fall off.) Strain out all water. At the same time, in a heavy skillet sauté garlic and potato in olive oil until tender. Return cabbage to large boiling pot and dump in garlic and potatoes. Add a little water if needed to make a more moist consistency and heat thoroughly. Taste and add salt if needed.

Don Rispoli

This dish can be put into a casserole dish and reheated, so it's great for potlucks. It goes especially well with pork.

BAKED VEGETABLES

Whole mushrooms
Bell peppers, cut in 1" squares
Onions, quartered
Broccoli florets
Cherry tomatoes
Zucchini
Butter
Seasoning salt
Chicken broth (optional)

These are perfect served over rice with grilled steak. Use whatever vegetables you like.

Use appropriate amounts of these or other vegetables for the number of people you are feeding. Put vegetables in a deep baking dish. Top with pats of butter and sprinkle with seasoning salt. You can use chicken broth instead of butter. Make sure you have enough liquid so vegetables don't bake onto your dish. Better to err on the side of more than less.

Cover tightly and bake at 425 F. for about 20-25 minutes.

Sheri Gotay

CORN PIE

1 1/4 cups saltine cracker crumbs
1/2 cup margarine, melted
1 1/2 cups milk
2 cups fresh or frozen corn (I like to use frozen
     corn with red and green peppers)
1/4 T. instant minced onion
1/2 tsp. salt
2 T. flour
2 eggs
Paprika
1/2 tsp. pepper

Serves 6.

Mix crumbs and melted margarine. Set aside about 1 cup. With spoon, press remaining crumbs into a 9" pie tin to form shell. In a saucepan, mix 1 cup milk, corn, salt, pepper and onion. Bring to a boil, reduce heat and simmer 3 minutes. Blend flour and remaining milk; stir into hot mixture and cook, stirring until thickened. Cool slightly. Gradually add eggs, stirring vigorously. Pour into pan and sprinkle with reserved crumbs and paprika. Bake at 400 F. for 15 minutes.

Karen Hayes

T his is a Thanksgiving dinner favorite.

Seattle, Washington

BANANES À LA MOUTARDE

8 bananas, peeled
8 thin slices of ham
Dijon mustard
1/4 cup butter
2 T. flour
2 cups cold milk
1/2 lb. Gruyère, cut in cubes
Dash of nutmeg
Salt and pepper to taste

Serves 8.

Badigeonner chaque tranche de jambon avec une grosse cuiller de moutarde, y enrouler la banane. Ranger les "rouleaux" dans un plat allant au four. Préparer une sauce béchamel: mettre 50 g. de beurre dans une casserole et le faire fondre doucement; ajouter 2 grosses cuillers de farine. Mouiller avec du lait froid et laisser cuire sur feu très doux sans cesser de battre avec un fouet. Saler et poivrer. Ajouter un peu de noix de muscade. Ajouter 150 g. de Gruyère coupé en dès. Couvrir les "rouleaux" avec cette sauce et cuire au four (a feu moyen) pendent une trentaine de minutes.

OR

Spread a huge spoonful of Dijon mustard on a ham slice and roll it around a banana. Put each roll in the bottom of a 10" x 14" ovenproof pan. Make a béchamel sauce: Melt 1/4 cup butter in a sauce pan. Add 2 big tablespoons of flour. Mix in 2 cups of cold milk and heat on low heat, stirring constantly with a whip until sauce thickens. Add salt, pepper and a bit of nutmeg if you wish. Add Gruyère cheese . When cheese melts, pour sauce over the banana-ham rolls and cook at 350 F. for 30 minutes.

Derry and Ski Sherensky

When we went to France to live in 1984, the first family to invite us to their home for dinner was the Descoing family. We were later to taste many delights from the hand of Eve Descoing, but my favorite will always be "Bananes à la Moutarde". Eve is an unofficial member of our houseboat dock family, having twice exchanged her home for a visit on our dock. This is our French entry to the cookbook, dedicated to Eve Descoing. It sounds strange, but you won't even know there are bananas in it — it's not sweet.

Bon appetit!

FRIED GREEN TOMATOES

2 medium-size hard green tomatoes
3-4 T. flour
1 egg
3-4 T. milk
Salt, pepper and cayenne to taste
Progresso Italian bread crumbs
Olive oil and butter (mix 50/50) for frying

Serves 2.

Cut tomatoes into 3/4" slices. If using end pieces, cut off skin on the
end. Put flour and tomatoes in a plastic bag and shake to coat slices.
Set slices on a cookie sheet or rack. Beat egg, milk, salt, pepper and
cayenne in shallow bowl. Heat butter and oil in frying pan on medium
heat until hot (but do not burn butter). Put bread crumbs on a plate.
Dip tomatoes in egg mixture, then dredge in crumbs to coat. Fry in
heated frying pan until brown, then turn and fry other side until brown.
Drain on a rack so bottom does not get soggy.

Jann McFarland

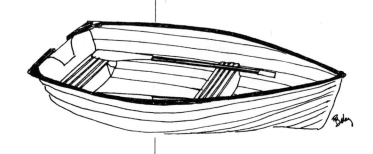

A typical day on Lake Union begins before dawn with the rowing crews shuttling up and down the lake, the coxswains' barks alerting the rest of us that it's time to arise. One or two pleasure boats slip quietly out, leaving the first small ripples. At 8:00 the first seaplanes taxi down the lake and take off for watery destinations such as the San Juan islands and Victoria. More pleasure boats, some work boats...the day proceeds. The harbor police make their rounds, ever alert for those exceeding the 7 knot speed limit or without current tax stickers and life preservers. A NOAA ship or fish processor may enter the lake before it gets too busy, moving ever so slowly, and tug boats drag everything from log booms to barges of sand and gravel

TAKEOFF TOFU

1 block tofu
1 egg, well beaten
Flour for dredging
Oil for frying
1/4 cup soy sauce
1 T. water
2 tsp. ginger, grated

Serves 8.

Drain liquid from tofu. Cut in 1" or 2" pieces. Dust each piece with flour and dip in egg. Dust again with flour. Fry tofu in hot oil. Remove from pan. Mix soy sauce and water and pour over tofu. Garnish with grated ginger. If you don't like tofu, throw it at a noisy seaplane.

Marty Gardner

HOMEMADE HOUSEBOAT AIRPLANE

13 years of dreams
10 years of saving dimes in a red airplane bank
1 supportive wife
1 supportive wife's checkbook
2 bedroom floating home
5 extraordinary friends
1 vacation to Oshkosh
Patience (mostly wife's)

First, get your private pilot license. Then marry a woman with the patience of Job who gives you a red airplane bank for your first Christmas together. Buy a lot of things that give you dimes as change so you can put them in your bank. Take a vacation with your wife to the world's largest airshow in Oshkosh, Wisconsin. Be sure to forget your checkbook, the depository of all those dimes. Find a Kit Fox (as in "build-it-yourself") airplane that you MUST have and get your supportive wife, who did not forget her checkbook, to pay for it.

Once back home, pay your wife back immediately so she quits calling it "her" airplane! Do not let your jaw drop when the "kit" which arrives is larger than any room in your houseboat. Knock out a few walls and windows, sacrifice a bedroom, and soon enough your workshop is ready! Now add the help of your extraordinary friends in moving all the pieces of the airplane puzzle into the "assembly hangar". Spend millions of hours organizing the zillions of pieces, from nuts and bolts to ailerons and wings. Keep promising your patient and supportive wife that this thing will fly, someday! Promise your patient and supportive wife that the house will look like a normal houseboat again — someday!

Susan "Job" Susor

or construction equipment. In the afternoon, brightly colored rental kayaks and canoes speckle the lake. If there is a good breeze there may be a wind surfer darting around amongst sailboats of all sizes. Many interesting and beautiful old craft come out of the Center for Wooden Boats. Motor boats, from tiny to ostentatious, abound. Five or six times a day the harbor tour boats chug down the lake, pointing out the sights over their loudspeakers. Young men try to impress (we guess) with their ever louder "cigarette" boats. In the evening, the party boats make the rounds, luminous and rocking with music. A distinctive steam whistle blast reminds us the historic Virginia V steamboat is still around. The lake quiets with the dusk.

SHRIMP CURRIED EGGS

8 hard boiled eggs, cut in half lengthwise

Filling:
1/3 cup mayonnaise
1/2 tsp. salt
1/2 tsp. paprika
1/2 tsp. curry powder
1/4 tsp. dry mustard

Sauce:
2 T. butter
2 T. all purpose flour
1 10 oz. can frozen condensed cream of shrimp soup, thawed
    (cream of mushroom or cream of chicken may be used)
10 oz. milk
1/2 cup shredded cheddar cheese
1 small can of shrimp, clams or crab (optional)

1 cup bread crumbs
1 T. margarine or butter, melted

Serves 6-8.

Remove yolks from eggs and mash. Mix yolks with mayonnaise, salt, paprika, curry powder and dry mustard. Refill egg whites with this mixture and place in 10" x 6" x 1 1/2" baking dish.

Melt 2 T. butter. Blend in flour. Add soup and milk. Cook until thick and bubbly. Add cheese and stir until melted. (Add extra shrimp, clams or crab if desired.) Cover eggs with this sauce.

Mix bread crumbs with 1 T. melted butter or margarine and sprinkle around edge of dish. Bake at 350 F. for 15-20 minutes.

Susan Chatlos-Susor

This isn't an original, but it's my husband's favorite and he asks that I make it often for potluck dinners. It's good and easy!

EGGS WESTLAKE

2 1/2 lbs. peeled, chopped, whole tomatoes
   (canned are fine, but drain them first)
2 T. sugar
8 eggs
Salt and pepper to taste

Serves 4 (2 eggs each).

In a large frying pan, simmer tomatoes, sugar, salt and pepper until mixture is semi-firm (liquid is gone). Stir frequently. Make a well for each egg. Crack an egg into each well.

Cover and cook on medium heat for about 4 minutes. Watch carefully so yolks don't harden. Serve eggs surrounded by tomatoes. Accompany with bagels.

Carol and Tim Kane

Houseboating is not for everyone. One morning our neighbor, Marcia, called for a taxi cab. Upon seeing her come up the steps from the dock, the driver, who was from another country, queried, "You live down there?" "Yes! We live on a houseboat," she replied enthusiastically.   "In my country," he observed, "we fled those kinds of places!"

DUCK FOOD

Breads

FAIRVIEW AVENUE HERB BREAD

3 cups flour
4 tsp. baking powder
1/4 cup brown sugar
1/4 tsp. thyme
1/4 tsp. rosemary
1/2 tsp. dill seed
1/2 tsp. caraway seed
1/2 tsp. celery seed
1/2 tsp. anise seed
1 tsp. salt
1 T. toasted sesame seeds
1/4 cup oil
1 1/4 cups milk
2 eggs, slightly beaten

This is a quick and easy recipe and is best served warm out of the oven.

Makes 1 loaf.

Sift together dry ingredients. Mix in remaining ingredients and beat well. Put in greased loaf pan. You can sprinkle sesame or poppy seeds on top. Bake at 350 F. for one hour.

Elissa Kamins

STORMY WEATHER BEER BREAD

12 oz. beer
3 T. sugar
3 cups self-rising flour
2 T. melted butter

Makes 1 loaf.

Preheat oven to 350 F. Grease loaf pan (approx. 9" x 5"). Mix ingredients and pour into prepared loaf pan. Bake 50 minutes, then brush top with butter. Bake 10 minutes more. Cool 10-15 minutes, remove from pan, enjoy.

M. Liz Crowell

Super fast! Super easy! Great for soups. This recipe is from my Aunt Gloria who lives on the stormy Oregon Coast where she and her family enjoy many nights at home with this bread and homemade soups.

*M*y neighbors were remodeling their houseboat. It was pretty much gutted, however their daughter was still "camping" there at night. The refrigerator remained, but had been moved to the center of the room to accommodate the carpenters. She kept cereal and bread on the top of it. One night she came home and found two raccoons dangling from the rafters trying to grab the plastic bread sack which remained just out of their reach.

Houseboat Old-timer

PULL-APART GARLIC BREAD

1 loaf frozen whole wheat or white bread dough,
   cut into 32 pieces
1/3 cup unsalted butter, melted
2 T. chopped fresh parsley
2 T. finely chopped onion
1 tsp. minced fresh garlic
1/4 tsp. salt

Serves 8-10.

Place bread dough pieces in a large bowl. Combine remaining ingredients in a small bowl. Pour over bread dough and toss to coat well. Arrange bread dough in greased 1 1/2 quart casserole. Cover and let rise in warm place until double in size (1 1/2-2 hours). Heat oven to 375 F. Bake for 30-35 minutes or until golden brown. If bread begins to brown too quickly, shield with aluminum foil. Cool 10 minutes; invert pan to remove bread. Serve warm.

June Fauchald

FISHING DERBY CORNBREAD

2 cups unbleached white flour
2 cups coarse grain cornmeal
8 tsp. baking powder
1 1/2 tsp. salt
4 eggs
1 1/2 cups milk
1/2 cup cream or half & half
1/2 cup melted butter
1/4 cup honey
1/4 cup molasses

Serves 15

Stir together dry ingredients. Add eggs, milk, cream, butter, honey, and molasses. Mix until all ingredients are well stirred, but don't over mix. Pour into 2 greased 9" x 9" x 2" pans or large pie plates. Bake at 425 F. for 20 to 25 minutes. Check after 15 minutes if using a different size pan.

Debra Boyer

After years of waiting and hoping George would bring home the winning salmon, something had to be done. This recipe was developed to fill the bellies of many hungry, disappointed and mean-spirited crowds. Goes best with butter and homemade jam.

7 CARD STUD SOFT PRETZELS

I don't remember who I stole this recipe from, but it's easy and that's what I like!

1 pkg. yeast
1 1/2 cups warm water
1/8 tsp. ginger
1 T. sugar
1 tsp. salt
4 cups flour
1 egg, beaten
Coarse salt

Dissolve yeast in the warm water, stir in the ginger. Add sugar and salt. Blend in flour. Dump the dough out and knead lightly on a floured board until smooth. Tear off 12-14 small pieces of dough and roll them into ropes. Then twist them into pretzel shapes. Put them on a lightly buttered cookie sheet. Brush with the beaten egg and sprinkle with coarse salt. Bake at 425 F. for 15 minutes until browned.

Sheri Lockwood

ORANGE LOAF

1 lb. orange jelly candy, cut in small pieces
1/2 lb. pitted dates
2 cups chopped walnuts
1 1/2 cups flaked coconut
1/2 cup flour
1 cup butter
2 cups sugar
4 eggs
1 tsp. baking soda
1/2 cup buttermilk

Glaze:
1 cup orange juice
2 cups powdered sugar

Makes 7 small loaves.

Combine candy, dates, walnuts and coconut. Mix together with flour and set aside. In another bowl, cream butter, sugar and eggs (one at a time) until light. Mix baking soda and buttermilk and add to butter mixture. Stir dry ingredients into creamed mixture. Pour into 7 small greased and floured loaf pans, about 2/3 full. Bake at 300 F. for 1 1/2 to 1 3/4 hours. Optional glaze can be added when loaves are cool. Mix orange juice and powdered sugar and drizzle on loaves. Refrigerate loaves overnight. Remove from pans and wrap to store.

Anna Brown

Remodeling a houseboat is different. Plumb bobs are useless when the house itself bobs. Flotation problems also cause trouble. Our house has been remodeled four times over 24 years, each time adding weight and, therefore, flotation. The last time we remodeled, the fact that we're in very shallow water by the shore caused some problems. The house was level when we moved back in, but when the lake started to rise to its summer level, we noticed that one side of the house did not — it was sitting on the bottom! That summer we learned to live at an angle. When Fall came and the lake level fell, so did one side of the house, while the other still sat on the bottom. Luckily there are professional "flotation management specialists" in our unique community who know how to handle just such problems!
Fred Bassetti

SWEET DOUGH YEAST BREAD

Dough:
1/2 cup warm water (105-115 F.)
2 pkgs. dry yeast
1 1/2 cups lukewarm milk
1/2 cup sugar
1 tsp. vanilla
2 tsp. salt
3 eggs
1/2 cup soft margarine or butter
7-7 1/2 cups sifted white flour
1-2 T. oil (to coat bowl)

Walnut filling:
1 1/2 lbs. walnuts, finely chopped (ground is best)
1/2 cup sugar
Honey to taste
Splash of milk

Lekvor filling:
1 jar Lekvor (prune jelly available at most large
    grocery stores)

Poppy seed filling:
3/4 cup poppy seed, ground fine
1/2 cup sugar
Honey to taste
Splash of milk

Makes 3 or 4 small loaves.

Put warm water in large mixing bowl and stir in yeast until completely dissolved. Add in the following order: milk, sugar, vanilla, salt, eggs, margarine or butter, and 1/2 of the flour. Mix thoroughly. Add the rest of the flour very slowly, mixing with a spoon until smooth. The dough should be able to be mixed easily with a spoon, then mix with your hands. Turn onto a lightly floured surface. Knead dough until smooth and elastic — about 5 minutes. Roll into a ball and place in a lightly

oiled bowl, coating the entire ball of dough with the oil from the bowl. Cover with a damp cloth and let rise in a warm (85 F.) place until dough doubles in size (about 1 1/2 hours). Punch down and let it rise again until almost doubled in size (about 30 minutes).

Divide into 3-4 portions. Roll each portion on a floured surface until 1/8-1/4 inch thick. Spread filling to cover the dough. Roll up and place on a greased cookie sheet. Let rise 30 minutes before baking. Brush top of dough with well-beaten egg before putting into 415 F. oven for 25-30 minutes.

For walnut and poppy seed fillings: Combine all ingredients and add just enough milk to make a thick, spreadable paste. Use Lekvor from the jar.

Susan Chatlos-Susor

SEE YOU AND RAISE YOU APPLESAUCE OATMEAL MUFFINS

This 190 calorie muffin recipe makes 24 hearty, low-fat breakfast muffins. It was given to me by a friend and is a proven success. She bakes them regularly, freezes them in small packages, and thaws them in a microwave — a pair every morning — for her husband, who never gets tired of them. They aren't very sweet — I like 'em.

3 cups oatmeal
2 1/2 cups flour
1 cup brown sugar
2 tsp. baking soda
2 tsp. baking powder
2 cups applesauce
2 tsp. cinnamon
2 eggs (use whites only if you want less cholesterol)
6 T. oil
1 cup lowfat milk

Topping:
2 T. butter
1/2 tsp. cinnamon
1/2 cup oatmeal

Makes 2 dozen.

Mix ingredients in whatever order pleases you. Heat oven to 400 F. Use non-stick muffin pans or grease regular muffin pans. Divide batter evenly into 24 muffins. Sprinkle with topping (optional) and bake 15 to 20 minutes. Test with toothpick for doneness. Crushed walnuts make a nice addition either to the batter or to the topping.

Caroline Callender from Ladies Poker Night

REFRIGERATOR BRAN MUFFINS

2 cups All Bran
2 cups boiling water
2 1/2 cups raisins (yellow sultanas)
4 eggs, slightly beaten
2 cups sugar
1 cup salad oil
1 cup wheat germ
4 cups bran flakes
1 quart buttermilk
1 T. baking soda
1 tsp. salt
4 cups flour
1 1/2 cups chopped walnuts

Makes 4-5 dozen muffins

Mix All Bran, boiling water and raisins in bowl and let cool. Mix baking soda and salt into flour. Add remaining ingredients to cooled All Bran and raisin mixture. Fill muffin cups full as mix does not rise excessively. Bake at 400 F. for 20 minutes.

Gwen Bassetti

This batter may be refrigerated for up to 6 weeks! Make just enough for breakfast and save the rest.

BANANA BLUEBERRY NUT BRAN MUFFINS

1 1/2 cups white sugar
4 ripe bananas, pureed
1 pkg. frozen blueberries
1 cup chopped walnuts
2 eggs
3 tsp. baking soda
1 1/2 tsp. vanilla
2 cups oat bran
1 quart buttermilk
4 cups Kellogg's All Bran
2 1/2 cups unsifted flour

Makes approximately 2 dozen muffins

Combine first 8 ingredients. Add remaining ingredients. Fill muffin tins 2/3 full and bake at 375 F. for 30 minutes.

Dick McMillen

BASIC "I HATE TO COOK" MUFFINS

1 cup beer
2 cups buttermilk baking mix

Makes 8-12 muffins.

Mix ingredients so you barely have a batter, but no more — don't beat it. Pour batter into greased muffin tins or cups. Bake at 400 F. for about 12 minutes.

June Fauchald

These muffins have a good sourdough taste, especially when they're hot from the oven. There will be a few ounces of beer left in the can, but I'm sure you can think of something to do with it!

BOAT STREET PUMPKIN BRAN MUFFINS

When I was a kid in the early fifties, my paper route included lots of houseboats. Often when I would go to collect my money, the houseboats would have been moved around, or, in some instances, completely disappeared.

Sid McFarland

2 cups white sugar
4 ripe bananas, puréed
1 29 oz. can pumpkin
2 eggs
1 cup chopped walnuts or raisins
4 1/2 tsp. baking soda
3 tsp. cinnamon
1 1/2 tsp. ground ginger
1 tsp. ground cloves
2 cups oat bran
1 quart buttermilk
4 cups Kellogg's All Bran
2 cups unbleached white flour

Makes approximately 2 dozen muffins.

Combine first 10 ingredients. Add remaining ingredients. Fill muffin tins 2/3 full and bake at 350 F. for 35 minutes.

Dick McMillen

LAND OF NOD CINNAMON BUNS

20 frozen dough rolls
1 cup brown sugar
1/4 cup vanilla instant pudding powder
1-2 T. cinnamon
1/4-1/2 cup melted butter

Makes 20 rolls.

Grease a 10" bundt pan. Place frozen dough rolls in pan. Sprinkle with brown sugar, pudding powder and cinnamon. Pour melted butter over all. Cover with a clean, damp cloth and leave at room temperature over night. In the morning, preheat oven to 350 F. and bake for 25 minutes. Let sit for 5 minutes and then turn out on a serving plate.

Karen Hayes

Your house will smell wonderful in the morning. If you make these rolls for company, you will be embarrassed to tell them how simple it is!

There are certain elements of construction that are unique to houseboats. We must deal with flotation, stringers, and underwater plumbing, sciences not taught in Homebuilding 101. Rather, expertise in these fields has been developed by trial and error over many years by a very select, and small group of people. We have our "flotation man", our "stringer man", and a man I call our "diving plumber" and jack of all trades. I doubt very much if there's a houseboat alive that has not at some point in its history been tended to by one of these unique individuals.

Marty Alexander

DANISH PUFF PASTRY

2 sticks (1/2 lb.) butter or margarine
2 cups flour
1 cup plus 3 T. ice water
1 tsp. almond extract
3 eggs

Frosting:
2 T. melted butter
1 T. hot water
1/2 tsp. almond extract
1/2 pkg. powdered sugar
Ground nuts as garnish

Makes 2 pastries.

Preheat oven to 375 F. Mix 1 stick of butter or margarine, 1 cup flour and 3 T. ice water into a pie crust dough (it will be sticky). Pat this out in 2 oval strips as wide as your cookie sheet, about 10" long by 5" wide. Put 1 stick of butter and 1 cup of water in a saucepan and bring to a boil. Add 1 cup flour and 1 tsp. almond extract and stir until it balls in the pan. Add eggs one at a time, beating after each is added. Spread this mixture over pie crust layers and bake at 375 F. for 40-55 minutes. Cool out of draft. Mix all frosting ingredients and frost after pastries are cool. Sprinkle with ground nuts.

Elaine Powell

EASY COFFEE CAKE

1 cup sour cream
1 tsp. baking soda
1/4 lb. butter
1 1/4 cups sugar
3 eggs, well beaten
1 tsp. vanilla
1 1/2 cups sifted cake flour
2 T. chopped nuts
2 tsp. cinnamon

Serves 12-15.

Mix sour cream and soda and let stand. Cream together the butter and 1 cup of the sugar. Add the eggs and vanilla. Stir in flour, alternating with sour cream mixture. Pour into greased 8" x 12" Pyrex baking dish. Top with mixture of nuts, cinnamon and 1/4 cup sugar. Bake in 350 F. oven for 35 minutes.

Ellen Hansen

PILING IT ON

Desserts

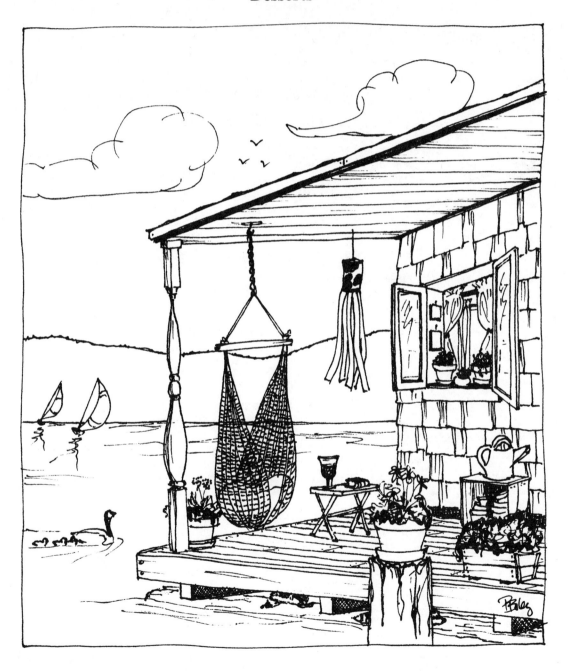

GEPETTO'S RICOTTA CHEESE PIE

W̲e had heavy rains and snow melt one year, flooding beavers out of their homes into the lake. In an effort to gather new wood to construct new dams (heaven knows where), trees and shrubs began to disappear off many of the decks. It was truly a unique sight to watch the beavers pulling trees down the channel in search of a spot to make a dam! (We lost a beautiful large rhododendron.)

Crust:
1/4 cup graham cracker crumbs (Oreo cookies are great too)
1/4 cup sugar
3/4 stick butter, melted

Filling:
1 1/2 pounds ricotta cheese
3/4 cup sugar
1 cup toasted chopped almonds
1 cup semisweet chocolate chips, ground slightly
1 T. almond extract
1 T. almond liqueur (optional)
1 cup whipped cream

Serves 12-16.

Mix graham cracker crumbs, sugar and melted butter. Press into a 10" springform pan and bake at 350 F. for 10 minutes.

Beat cheese and sugar in food processor. Add nuts and chocolate chips and blend until they are in small chunks. Add flavorings. Whip cream and gently fold into cheese mixture. Pour into cooled crust and refrigerate several hours.

Theresa Harvey

MOTHER'S CREAM CHEESE PIE

Crust:
1 pkg. Graham Crackers
3/4 cube melted margarine or butter

Filling:
15 oz cream cheese
1/2 cup sugar
1/2 tsp. vanilla
2 eggs

Topping:
1/2 pint sour cream
2 T. sugar
1 tsp. vanilla

A certain success!

Serves 6-8.

Mix crushed graham crackers and melted butter in 9" pie pan. Press firmly along sides and bottom to make crust.

Beat filling ingredients well, pour into pie pan, bake in pre-heated 275 F. oven for 20 minutes. Remove. Heat oven to 450 F. Mix topping ingredients and pour over pie, covering top completely. Put back in oven and bake at 450 F. for 5 minutes. Cool and chill well.

Michael McCrackin

FALL HARVEST PIE

This is a pie I have enjoyed sharing with friends, and it has a subtle and intriguing flavor. I was fortunately able to have access to my neighbor's wild apples and Italian prune plums and an adjacent wild blackberry bank. If you have access to blueberries or huckleberries, they can replace or mix in with the blackberries.

3 small wild apples or 2 cups sliced peeled tart apples
1/2 cup blackberries (fresh or frozen)
1/2 cup peeled pitted wild prune plums
1/4 cup red seedless grapes & golden raisins
1/4 cup melted butter and additional soft butter
1/4 cup walnuts or hazelnuts coarsely chopped
1/4 tsp. grated orange rind
1 T. chopped candied ginger
1/2 to 2/3 cup brown or raw sugar
1/8 tsp. mace
Pinch of salt
1 T. minute tapioca
1 T. cornstarch
1 egg white
Pie dough for one 10" bottom & top or strips for lattice top*

Serves 10-12.

Assemble all the fresh fruit and mix with raisins, orange rind, ginger and nuts. Brush with melted butter and sprinkle tapioca over bottom of pie crust in a 9" springform pan. Spread mixed fruit evenly in pie shell.

Combine sugar, mace, pinch of salt and cornstarch and sift over fruit until coated and mix lightly. Dot with additional bits of butter. Cover with top crust, sprinkle with a little sugar and brush with egg white. Bake in preheated oven at 450 F. for 10 minutes, reduce heat to 350 F. for 45 minutes to an hour until the smell reaches out to you!

Caroline Culbertson

*See recipe for "Harvest Pie Crust".

HARVEST PIE CRUST

2 ounces whole hazelnuts
1 3/4 cups all purpose flour
1/2 cup confectioners sugar
1/2 tsp. grated lemon zest
1/2 tsp. cinnamon
1/2 cup (1 stick) unsalted butter, cold, cut into small bits
1 large egg, lightly beaten

Heat oven to 375 F.

Toast hazelnuts on baking sheet 8-10 minutes. Rub nuts together in clean kitchen towel to remove skins. Let cool. Process until finely ground in blender or food processor. Measure 1/2 cup ground nuts. Process nuts, flour, sugar, lemon peel and cinnamon in processor just to combine, about 10 seconds. Scatter butter on top and blend until mixture resembles coarse crumbs. Measure 1 1/2 tablespoons of egg and set aside for glazing pie. Drizzle remaining egg over pastry and process just until gathered into a rough ball. Shape dough into thick disk and refrigerate, wrapped in plastic wrap, 30 minutes. (You can make the pie filling while dough is chilling.)

Roll out 2/3 of the pastry into a 12 inch circle. Trim edge. Press pastry into bottom and up side of 9 inch springform pan. Roll remaining 1/3 pastry into 9-10 inch circle. Cut into ten 1/2 inch wide strips for lattice top. Freeze strips 3-5 minutes on baking sheet to firm.

Spoon filling into pastry and smooth top. Lift pastry strips off baking sheet with table knife. Arrange strips 1 1/2 inches apart in lattice on top of filling. Fold excess at edge onto filling.

To make decorative crimped edge: Press remaining three strips around edge to make continuous smooth edge, trimming as needed. Insert thin metal spatula between pastry and side of pan and push pastry slightly away from edge of pan; continue all around edge. Place end of thin wooden spoon or chopstick on inside edge of pastry, place fingers on outside edge, and push pastry with spoon into fingers to crimp it. Repeat around edge.

Brush lattice and edge with reserved egg. Bake until pastry is golden brown, 40-45 minutes. Cool on wire rack 10-20 minutes. Remove side of pan and let cool completely before serving.

Caroline Culbertson

If you are short of time, I have found that very good crust can be made by using a packaged pie crust mix and mixing the nuts, lemon zest and cinnamon into the dough, following the directions on the pie crust package. Fill this pie crust with "Fall Harvest Pie" filling for an incredible treat!

CHRISTMAS CRUISE APPLE PIE

I serve this every year at our
gathering to watch the Christmas
boats to screams of delight from
participants. It has long been the
centerpiece of my reputation as a
cook, a reputation which will surely
disintegrate when people discover
that it's really not so hard. Certain
individuals, who, except for Lucile
Flanagan, shall remain nameless,
have threatened to send me
swimming after the Christmas boats
if I don't put it in the book. In
revenge, I am giving all the details
so certain nameless people can do
it themselves. Besides, even "water
boilers" need one spectacular
specialty.

Filling:
4 to 5 Granny Smith or,
    if you can find them, Criterion apples
1 2 lb. can Freestone peaches, sliced
1/2 cup raisins (optional)
1/2 cup sugar mixed with
    1/2 tsp. cinnamon and 1/4 tsp. nutmeg
1 squeeze lemon

Crust:
2 cups all-purpose flour
1 tsp. salt
1/2 cup shortening
6 T. ice water

Serves 3 pigs, 8 polite guests.

The trick to the filling is to buy the right varieties of fruit. Some varieties aren't good. Delicious apples get dry and mushy when cooked. Gravenstein apples and Elberta peaches disintegrate. The Criterion apples are perfect, but hard to find. Firm, crispy fruit is best.

Peel the apples, take out the core, and slice them the same size as the peaches. Put apples in a bowl, squeeze the lemon over them and stir to keep them from turning brown. Drain the peaches (do a sloppy job so about 1/4 to 1/2 cup of the juice stays in the can). Put the peaches, juice and raisins in the bowl of apples. Stir it up. Sprinkle the sugar mixture over the top. Stir it some more. You can adjust the amount of sugar and cinnamon to suit your own tastes. Set aside. The longer it "stews", the better it is. Oh, turn the oven to 425 F., so it'll be nice and hot at baking time.

Measure the flour, salt, and shortening. When measuring Crisco, pack it down tight so there aren't any little air pockets lousing up the measurement. Put the Crisco in the freezer for about 5 minutes to firm it up a little.

Note: Beginners should use a 9" pie pan. The crust will be a little thicker and easier to roll out. After a little practice, you can make 13-inchers.

Cutting the Fat and Flour:

Find a deep and not-too-wide mixing bowl. (I use one that's 5" deep and 7" wide.) Pour in flour. Sprinkle salt across the top and stir with a spoon to mix. Dump the Crisco in the middle of the flour and cut the Crisco into, say, 20 pieces. Get another kitchen knife. Now cut one knife across another (in the middle of the flour and Crisco pieces, not in mid-air). Keep "scissoring", stopping occasionally to move the dry flour from the edge of the bowl to your cutting area for 5 to 10 minutes.

The object is to cut the flour and Crisco together until you have a lot of little 1/8" to 1/4" pea-sized balls of Crisco coated with flour. When you roll out the crust, these flatten out layering on top of one another to make flakes for a flakey crust. You can add a little extra Crisco if you can't seem to get enough little balls. Don't cut so much that the balls get too small. When most of it is the right size, grab handfuls and squeeze it gently together, then crumble it apart into the bowl. This will pick up any stray flour and attach it to some Crisco somewhere.

Now pile the dough on one side of the bowl. Sprinkle a little of the ice water on it. With a fork toss the dampened part of the dough to the empty side of the bowl. Keep doing this until all the water is used up. Then stir gently to evenly distribute the water throughout the dough. Divide the dough in half and firmly press each half into a ball. Cover each with plastic wrap and put it in the refrigerator for 1/2 hour or so.

Rolling Out the Dough:

The trick in rolling out crusts is to use just enough flour to keep things from sticking, but not so much that you dry it out.

Find a big (at least 1' x 1') area of the kitchen (a piece of tinfoil on the floor is okay; the top of the hot stove is not) and sprinkle about 1/2 cup flour on it. Spread the flour around with your hand to make sure the whole 1 foot area is coated with flour. Dust some flour on the rolling pin.

Take one of the dough balls and flatten it out a little with the palm of your hand. Drag it around the floured area to coat its backsides with flour.

Turn it over and drag it around a little more. Now roll it out. Start at the middle and roll towards the edges. Roll about 1/2" beyond the edge with each stroke. Don't pound it! It's your baby; be gentle. Turn it occasionally to stop sticking. Sprinkle on a little flour when needed.

The Christmas Boat Parade is one of the highlights of the holiday season in Seattle if you happen to live near the water. Participants decorate their boats with lights and music — some are very elaborate! Every night for a week they entertain a different shoreline — Lake Union, Lake Washington, Elliott Bay, Shilshole, West Seattle. People celebrate in homes along the route, and from the docks and beaches if it's not too cold.

Gently fold the crust in half being careful not to crack it in the middle. (If it sticks, use a spatula to gently pry up the sticky place.) Slide it onto the pie tin and unfold it. Very gently press it into the bottom of the tin, just so the crust and tin make contact. Repair any cracks using drops of cold water as glue. Lots of cracks means you used too much flour during rolling. Use less next time.

Now pour in the filling. Put three pats of butter on the top. Roll out the top crust and lay it over the top. Pinch the top and bottom crusts together around the edge of the pie. If they won't stick, use a few drops of water as glue. Run a knife around the outside edge of the tin to cut off any excess dough. Make about 8 holes in the top for steam. Punch them with a fork or knife or cut fancy patterns. Sprinkle about a tsp. of sugar on the top to give it "sparkle".

Line a cookie sheet with tinfoil and put your pie on top. This distributes the heat evenly and catches drips. Put 'er in the hot oven and bake at 425 F. for 15 minutes. Turn the oven down to 350 F. and bake for 35 to 40 minutes until the crust is just golden brown. Cool for at least 5 minutes before you gobble it up.

Beth Means

MAPLE-CRANBERRY APPLE PIE

Filling:
4 cups cranberries
1 cup sugar
1/3 cup maple syrup
1/2 tsp. cinnamon
1/2 tsp. maple flavoring
1/8 tsp. salt
5 large Golden Delicious apples, peeled, halved and cored
3 T. unbleached flour

Cinnamon Crust:
2 1/4 cups unbleached flour
9 T. chilled vegetable shortening
9 T. chilled unsalted butter, cut into 6 pieces
1 T. sugar
3/4 tsp. cinnamon
3/4 tsp. salt
9 T. ice water (plus or minus)
2 T. unsalted butter, cut into pieces

Glaze:
1 large egg yoke
1 T. whipping cream

*W*hile *replacing the joists in my kitchen I was completely without a floor in that room for a time. Arriving home late one night, I found an otter with his little head poking up where the floor used to be!*

Filling: Combine cranberries, sugar and maple syrup in heavy skillet. Cook over medium heat until cranberries pop and mixture thickens, about 20 minutes. Keep stirring. Remove from heat. Add cinnamon, maple flavoring and salt and mix thoroughly. Slice apples, and combine with cranberry mixture. Add flour and once again mix thoroughly.

Crust: Add dry ingredients for crust along with shortening and butter and add enough water to bring dough together. Separate into 2/3 and 1/3 balls and chill dough in plastic bag. Prepare dough for 9 inch pie plate and spoon cranberry-apple mixture into prepared pie plate. Dot mixture with remaining two tablespoons of butter. Place rolled smaller piece of dough over filling and seal edges. Be sure to vent top. Glaze top with whisked egg white and whipping cream.

Bake for 10 minutes at 400 F. then reduce heat to 375 F. and cook for 50 minutes. Serve hot or at room temperature with whipped cream or your favorite ice cream.

Bob Williams

Seattle, Washington

BERRY FRESH PIE

4 cups blueberries
1/2 cup sugar
2 1/2 T. cornstarch
6 T. water
1 T. lemon juice
4 oz. cream cheese, softened
1 cup raspberries
1 9" pie shell, baked and cooled
Lots of whipped cream

*T*he Pacific Northwest is known for its wonderful abundance of berries. There are lots of places around Seattle to go to pick your own blueberries, or you can go up into the mountains and steal the blue huckleberries from the bears!

Serves 6-8.

In a saucepan, combine 2 cups of the blueberries with the sugar, corn-starch and water. Bring to a boil over medium-low heat and cook slowly until thickened, stirring constantly. This will take about 2 minutes. Remove from heat and add the lemon juice and then cool.

Spread the softened cream cheese carefully on the bottom of the pie crust. Stir 1 1/2 cups of the blueberries into the cooked and cooled blueberry mixture and pour into the pie shell. Sprinkle the raspberries and the remaining blueberries on top. Chill completely for about two hours.

Serve with lots of whipped cream.

Kirvil Skinnerland

CRANBERRY, APPLE, NUT, RAISIN PIE

2 cups cranberries, whole or chopped
2 cups apples, peeled and chopped
1 cup raisins
1 to 1 1/2 cups sugar
1/2 cup chopped nuts
2 T. quick cooking Tapioca
1/2 tsp. ground cinnamon

Pastry for 9" double crust pie
Milk optional

Serves 6-8.

Prepare pastry for 9" pie shell and chill.

Combine cranberries, apples, sugar, nuts, raisins, tapioca and cinnamon. Let stand 20 minutes.

Place bottom crust into pie pan. Turn cranberry mixture into pastry. Adjust top crust, pinch edges and vent top.

Brush top with milk, sprinkle with sugar, cover edges with foil to prevent burning. Bake at 375 F. for 25 minutes. Remove foil and continue to bake 25-30 minutes. Remove from oven and cool.

Bob Williams

When we first moved in, I was carrying 3 trays as I ran down the dock. Being new to the dock, I didn't remember the bend and, not being able to see because of the trays, walked right off the edge into the chilly December water of Lake Union. I lost the trays right away, but my bigger problem was that no one heard my calls for help, and the dock was too high to get out of the water. Nary a ladder in sight. Nor could I find a boat low enough to hoist out on. Fortunately I had several layers of clothes on. Finally I swam under the dock and made it to shore. The next day Tom dove for the trays, salvaging the two metal ones. Several months later I was having tea with a neighbor when she said, "You know, the strangest thing happened awhile ago. A beautiful wooden tray came floating by one day...."

Cork Foster

PORTAGE BAY LEMON PIE

2 large lemons
2 cups sugar
4 eggs, well beaten
Pastry for two crust pie

Serves 6-8.

Slice lemons thin as paper, rind and all. Combine with sugar and mix well. Let stand at least two hours, blending occasionally. Add beaten eggs to lemon mixture and mix well. Pour filling into pastry-lined 9" pie pan, arranging lemon slices evenly. Cover with top crust. Cut several slits near center.

Bake at 450 F. for 15 minutes. Reduce heat to 375 F. for 20 minutes, or until silver knife comes out clean. Cool before serving.

Mack Hopkins

Sugar-Free Sweet Potato Pie

3 yams, baked, peeled and mashed
2 eggs, well beaten
1 tsp. vanilla
1 tsp. cinnamon
1/2 tsp. nutmeg
2 T. melted butter
1/4-1/2 cup chopped walnuts (optional)
1/4-1/2 cup raisins (optional)
1 9" pie pastry

Serves 6-8.

Set oven at 350 F. Mix all ingredients (except walnuts and raisins). Run through a blender or food processor. (This step may be omitted, but I prefer the smoother texture.) Then mix in chopped walnuts and/or raisins (or they can be sprinkled on top for decoration). Place mixture into pie shell, bake until slightly brown or about 30 minutes. If it cooks too fast, place a sheet of foil over the top. If you would rather have a pudding, put mixture into a buttered baking dish and bake according to same directions.

Peg Boley

Sitting staring out my window one rainy November day, watching the dock's raccoon family boldly strutting by, striking dread in the timid hearts of my neighbor's kitties, I contemplated how I might enjoy the upcoming holiday dinner table extravaganza without breaking down and shoveling a scrumptious, luscious dessert into my ravaged, deprived body — without having a major medical reaction to what I love most, sugar! I'm allergic to it. Every holiday season is a crisis at mealtime. I came up with the idea of sweet potatoes. This recipe has saved me from sitting on my hands at every occasion. It has even gained popularity and I'm now asked to bring this pie to each holiday gathering. I now use yams as they seem to be sweeter.

My houseboat was one of the half dozen or so lost or destroyed as a result of the monopoly on moorages which developed due to environmental regulations passed in the early 1970's. Except for roughly 500 houseboat moorages in Seattle, state law now prohibits permanent over-water residential uses. In 1980, my moorage owner decided to evict me and move his own rental houseboat into my spot. The local law said he couldn't do it. With the backing of the Floating Homes Association, my wife, Caryl, and I decided to stand and fight. The case eventually made it to the State Supreme Court, where the law we'd depended upon was struck down in the summer of 1983. We were required to leave within days after the decision. Eviction day was dark indeed. Neighbors showed up to witness the event from all over the lake. The media had been following the case closely, and the dock was

RHUBARB CREAM PIE

1 1/2 cups sugar
3 T. flour
1/2 tsp. nutmeg
1 T. butter
2 eggs, well beaten
3 cups chopped rhubarb
2 pastry crusts for 9" pie pan

Serves 6-8.

Line a 9" pie pan with pastry crust. In a mixing bowl, blend sugar, flour, nutmeg and butter. Add eggs and beat until smooth. Spread rhubarb in pie plate over crust, then pour filling over rhubarb. Cover with top crust or lattice strips. Bake at 450 F. for 10 minutes, then at 350 F. for 30 minutes.

Hazel Nigh

PEANUT BUTTER PIE

Crust:
1 cup graham cracker crumbs
3 T. cocoa powder
3 1/2 T. sugar
3 T. flour
3 T. melted butter
Pinch cinnamon

Filling:
1/2 lb. cream cheese
1 cup smooth peanut butter
1 cup sugar
1 T. melted butter
1 1/2 tsp. vanilla
1 1/2 cups heavy cream

Topping:
3 oz. melted milk chocolate
1 1/2 T. salad oil
1/4 cup chopped peanuts

Serves 6-8.

Mix crust ingredients together and press firmly in a 9" pie pan. Chill until ready to fill.

Cream the cream cheese, peanut butter, sugar and butter together until smooth. Blend in vanilla and heavy cream. Pour filling into prepared pie crust, smoothing the top. Chill at least 3 hours.

In a double boiler, thin the melted chocolate with salad oil over low heat. Then spread quickly over top of the pie. Garnish with chopped peanuts. Return to refrigerator until chocolate sets.

Jennifer Hansen

crawling with television crews and reporters. The police were out in force with their largest boat in the water and a couple patrol cars up on the road. Finally, a tugboat hired by our moorage owner appeared. Houseboaters huddled in glum groups as they watched the tugboat crew disconnect our home's moorage lines and utilities and tow it over to the shore where they tied it up to an old apple tree. It was as if everyone knew that some moorage owners would soon press their advantage in the regulatory vacuum. In fact, only a few weeks passed before whole docks were served with eviction notices. People wouldn't feel secure again for years. We had two weeks to get out of the city limits. We put an ad in the paper. Somebody from Friday Harbor offered us a few thousand dollars, and we took it. The house is still in use there as a marina office.

Bill Keasler

"QUICK AND EASY" HOUSEBOAT BIRTHDAY CAKE

One of the first times I made this cake was for my son's half birthday party. Being 6 months old, he really didn't care for a gourmet cake, but all of his houseboat dock "aunts and uncles" were eager to be invited and enjoy it for him.

Cake:
1 T. unsalted butter
Flour
6 oz. semi-sweet chocolate chips
1 heaping T. instant coffee dissolved in
    2 T. boiling water
3 eggs
1/2 cup granulated sugar
2/3 cup cake flour, sifted
3 1/2 T. softened unsalted butter
Pinch of salt
1/8 tsp. cream of tartar
1 T. sugar

Cream filling:
4 egg yolks
2/3 cup sugar
1/2 cup hot milk
3/4 lb. softened unsalted butter
1 T. vanilla

Chocolate Glaze:
1/4 cup hot coffee
6 oz. semi-sweet chocolate chips

Serves 8-12.

About 4 days ahead, read recipe and take nap.

Cake: Preheat oven to 350 F. Butter and flour 8" round cake pan. Melt chocolate, coffee, and water. Stir and cool to tepid.

Separate eggs. Gradually beat 1/2 cup of sugar into egg yolks; beat until mixture is thick and a light yellow color. Gently mix in chocolate mixture and softened butter.

Beat egg whites until foamy. Beat in salt and cream of tartar. Continue beating until soft peaks are formed. Sprinkle in 1 T. sugar and beat until stiff peaks are formed.

Stir gently, with lifting motion, 1/4 cup egg whites into chocolate mixture; when partially blended, add 1/4 cake flour. Follow by adding 1/3
egg white and then 1/3 flour. Continue folding in these proportions
until all egg whites and flour are gone.

Pour into cake pan. Set on middle shelf of oven. Bake 25-30 minutes.
Let cool 5 minutes. Remove to cake rack.

Cream Filling: Beat egg yolks, gradually add sugar until thick and light
in color. Gradually beat in hot milk. Turn into sauce pan and stir over
moderate heat until thick enough to coat wooden spoon. Set pan in
cold water until lukewarm. With electric mixer gradually beat in butter.
Mixture will probably go through a grainy-looking stage, but keep
beating until smooth. Beat in vanilla.

Cut cake horizontally into 2 layers. Frost bottom layer with 1/2 cream
mixture. Set remaining cake layer on top. Frost top with remaining
cream mixture; mound in the middle to form rounded top. Refrigerate.

Chocolate Glaze: Melt chocolate in hot coffee. Stir until blended.
Pour over cold cake.

Present and serve only after fanfare of trumpets! (Very thin slices since
this cake is very rich.)

Linda Knight

This is almost fool-proof, dirties just one pan, doesn't need icing and is lots of fun to make with the help of a five or six year old.

KID KAKE

1 1/2 cups flour
3 T. cocoa
1 tsp. baking soda
1 cup sugar
1/2 tsp. salt
5 T. salad oil
1 T. vinegar
1 tsp. vanilla
1 cup cold water

In a square 8"x 8" baking pan, mix dry ingredients with a fork until they are thoroughly combined. Then make a hole in the center. Pour into the hole the salad oil, vinegar, vanilla and water. Stir with a fork until smooth. Be sure to get the corners. Be sure to taste the batter. Bake for 30 minutes at 350 F. Eat warm (five year olds can't wait) or cool.

Beth Means

MRS. MIDDLETON'S BLUEBERRY CAKE

2 1/2 cups sugar
1 cup shortening
3 eggs, well beaten
5 cups sifted flour
5 tsp. baking powder
1 tsp. salt
1 cup milk
1 1/2 pints blueberries
1 T. cinnamon

Serves 15-18.

Save out a little sugar to sprinkle over the blueberries. Cream together sugar and shortening until fluffy. Add eggs. Sift together dry ingredients and add to creamed mixture alternately with milk. Fold in blueberries. Pour mixture in greased 9" x 13" pan. Sprinkle with sugar and cinnamon. Bake at 350 F. for about 1 hour.

June Fauchald

This luscious recipe dates back to the 18th century. Made for the family of a New England sea captain in the 1870's, it was updated at that time to include the "new fangled baking powder".

A few years ago my dock had a summer party to beat all parties. In addition to a rummage sale (all proceeds to the dock party fund) and a contest for the best potluck dish (first prize: a gourmet food basket), we had a "lip sync" contest. We connected rafts across the channel between our two docks, constructed a stage, complete with curtains, and had a fabulously theatrical woman — a vaudeville star of old — act as the MC. The costumes were imaginative, and the song choices, well.... Highlights were: the winning act, a Latin number with the usually-demure Rich dressed in tight black pants and grinding like Elvis between colorfully-clad dancers, Cathy and Elizabeth;

(cont'd next page)

PINEAPPLE CARROT CAKE

1 1/2 cups salad oil
3 eggs
2 cups sugar
2 1/2 cups flour
1 tsp. salt
2 tsp. baking soda
2 tsp. cinnamon
2 tsp. vanilla
1 cup crushed pineapple, drained
1 cup shredded coconut
1 cup grated carrot
1 cup chopped nuts

Buttermilk frosting:
1/2 cup sugar
1/2 cup buttermilk
1/2 cup butter
1 tsp. baking soda
1 T. corn syrup
1 tsp. vanilla

Serves 15-18.

Mix oil, eggs and sugar in large bowl. Stir in flour, salt, baking soda and cinnamon and blend well. Add vanilla, pineapple, coconut, carrot and nuts. Blend well. Pour into well-greased and floured 9" x 13" baking pan. Bake at 350 F. for 45-50 minutes. When cake is done, put pan on a rack and prick cake all over with a fork.

While cake is baking, prepare frosting. Combine all ingredients in saucepan and bring to a boil. Cook over low heat for 5 minutes. Pour frosting over hot cake.

Hazel Nigh

APPLE CAKE

1 cup sugar
1/2 cup butter
1 egg
1 tsp. vanilla
3 large apples, peeled and chopped
1/2 cup chopped walnuts
1 cup + 1 T. flour
1 tsp. baking soda
Pinch of salt
1 tsp. cinnamon
1/2 tsp. nutmeg
Powdered sugar or whipped cream for topping

Serves 9.

Cream sugar and butter. Add egg and vanilla. Sift and add dry ingredients; then add apples and nuts and mix well. Bake in a greased, floured 8" or 9" square pan at 350 F. for 30-50 minutes. While warm sprinkle lightly with powdered sugar, or serve cooled with whipped cream.

Kris Eaton

Rich's elderly mother, visiting from Florida, coifed in long white braids and dressed in 1960's white "go-go" boots and a red vinyl mini-skirt, singing "These Boots Are Made For Walking" (and, prompted by the words, "one of these days these boots are gonna walk all over you", stomping on a large picture of the Ayatolla); and Dave and Marty singing "Make Believe" from the musical "Show-boat" — only we think the skinny legs on the pregnant girl were Dave's and the mustache on the guy was fake. Luckily the event was videotaped, because no one would believe it otherwise!

Marty Alexander

OLD FASHIONED GINGERBREAD

Nothing compares to a slice of hot gingerbread smothered with whipping cream, especially on those wet and gray winter days for which Seattle is famous.

1 cup boiling water
1/2 cup butter
1 cup molasses
2 1/2 cups flour
1/2 cup sugar
1 tsp. baking soda
1 tsp. ginger
1/2 tsp. cinnamon
1/2 tsp. cloves
1 egg
Whipped cream

Serves 12-16.

Pour boiling water over the butter and stir until it is melted. Then stir in the molasses. Mix together the dry ingredients and then add to the molasses mixture. Beat only until blended. Add the egg and beat until smooth.

Pour into a greased and floured 10" fluted pan. Bake at 350 F. for 50 minutes. Serve with whipped cream.

Kirvil Skinnerland

CANADIAN WAR CAKE

1 1/2 cups brown sugar (packed)
1/2 cup white sugar
2 cups hot water
1 cup raisins
1 cup walnuts
4 T. shortening
1 tsp. each salt, nutmeg and cinnamon
3/4 tsp. ground cloves
3 cups sifted flour
2 tsp. baking soda (dissolved in 1 T. water)

Boil all ingredients except flour and baking soda for 5 minutes. Cool. Add flour and soda. Bake in a lightly greased cake pan in a slow oven (300 to 325 F.) for about 1 hour and 15 minutes.

Dorothy Humber

This recipe has been in the family for many years. The "War Cake" refers to World War I. It keeps well (through a whole war if you hide it) and is better when several days old.

GRANDPA DAN'S FAVORITE PINEAPPLE UPSIDE DOWN CAKE

When Mike McCrackin and I got together, he took over all the cooking. Believe me, it's like dying and going to heaven when someone cooks for you! So after 29 years and 4 kids, I forsook the fine art of cooking (not, however, the eating!!). This is the recipe for my father's favorite dessert which, no doubt you have already guessed, Mike bakes.

1/3 cup melted butter
1/2 cup brown sugar
1 10-13 oz. can sliced pineapple (or fresh)
2 eggs
2/3 cup sugar
6 T. pineapple juice
1 tsp. vanilla
1 cup flour
1/3 tsp. baking powder
1/4 tsp. salt

Serves 8.

Topping: Put melted butter in 12 to 14 inch cast iron skillet (preferably enameled). Sprinkle brown sugar evenly over butter. Arrange fruit over brown sugar mix to cover bottom of pan. (You can also add pecan halves or maraschino cherries.)

Cake: Beat eggs 5 minutes. Beat in sugar, then add juice and vanilla. Beat. Sift together the flour, baking powder and salt. Add to batter. Stir and pour over fruit. Bake at 350 F. for 45 minutes. Invert cake onto large plate.

Roseann Ursino

END-MOORAGE DREAM CAKE

1 pkg. yellow cake mix
1 small pkg. coconut instant pudding mix
5 eggs
1 cup hot (tap) water
1/2 cup vegetable oil
1/4 cup poppy seeds
1 tsp. lemon extract

Serves 12-16.

Grease and flour a bundt pan. Mix all ingredients together, pour in pan and bake at 350 F. for 40-45 minutes.

Barbara Carstens

Each houseboat has its own colorful history. Often, in the process of remodeling, when a wall is torn out or a floor pulled up, clues are found. Old newspapers, which were often the only insulation in the old houseboats, reveal the date of the last remodel, and household products and antique bottles are discovered in hidden nooks behind walls and under floorboards.

Houseboat Old-timer

BOOTLEGGERS' RUM CAKE

2 qts. rum
1 cup butter
1 tsp. sugar
2 large eggs
1 cup dried fruit
1 tsp. soda
1 tsp. lemon juice
1 tsp. brown sugar
1 tsp. nuts
1 tsp. baking powder

Serves 12.

Before you start, sample the rum to check for quality (Good, isn't it?). Select a large mixing bowl, measuring cup, etc. Check the rum again — it must be just right. To be sure rum is of the highest quality, pour one cup of rum into a glass and drink it as fast as you can. Repeat. With an electric mixer, beat one cup of butter in a large fluffy bowl. Add one seaspoon of thugar and beat again. Meanwhile, make sure that the rum is of the highest quality. Try another cup. Open the second quart if necessary. Add 2 large eggs, 2 cups fried fruit and beat till high. If druit gets stuck in beaters, just pry it loose with drewscriber. Sample the rum again, checking for tonscisticity. Next, sift 3 cups pepper or salt (it really doesn't matter which). Sample the rum again. Sift 1/2 pint of lemon juice. Fold in chipped butter and strained nuts. Add 1 babblespoon of brown thugar, or whatever color you can find. Wix mel. Grease oven and turn cake pan to 350 gredees. Now pour the whole mess into the coven and ake. Check the rum again and go to bed.

Bootlegger Still in Exile

Some houseboats had trap doors to enable the bootleggers to escape from the Feds. One houseboat even has a secret hallway leading to a hidden room.

DRUNKEN PRUNE MOUSSE

12 oz. dried, pitted prunes, chopped fine
4 oz. cognac
3 oz. strong, cold tea
2 cups whipping cream
18 oz. bittersweet chocolate, chips or block
6 egg yolks
1/8 cup sugar
4 egg whites
Fresh strawberries or other berries
Whipped cream (optional)

Serves 10.

Combine prunes, cognac and tea and marinate overnight. Line a 3 quart form, round or oblong, with plastic and put in freezer. Whip 2/3 cup of whipping cream until stiff, and spread in bottom of frozen form; put back in freezer.

Melt chocolate in large bowl. Combine egg yolks and sugar and beat until porous. Stir egg yolks mixture into chocolate. Add the prunes and marinade to the chocolate mixture. Beat remaining 1 1/3 cups whipping cream until stiff; then mix into chocolate mixture. Beat egg whites until stiff. Beat about a third of the egg whites into chocolate mixture. Fold in remaining egg whites.

Pour mixture into frozen form and put back into freezer for a minimum of 6 hours. Turn mousse onto serving plate and remove plastic wrap. Cut into 1/2" slices and serve with strawberries or other berries and whipped cream if desired. Keeps up to a month in the freezer.

Surain af Sandeberg

I got this recipe out of the family treasury to celebrate the great Thanksgiving Day Windstorm of 1984 which caused "waves to the tops of houseboats", or so I've heard. We were on vacation, but the waves have gotten higher with each storyteller. I figure the place must have looked like a mousse when it was all over, even though it was suspiciously clean by the time we got back.

THANKSGIVING WINDSTORM MOUSSE

1/2 cup sweet or semi-sweet chocolate bits
3 eggs, separated
1 tsp. vanilla

Serves 4.

Melt chocolate bits in double boiler. (Use hot, not boiling water in the lower pan.) Remove. Add egg yolks and beat. Add vanilla. In separate bowl, beat egg whites until stiff but not dry. Fold chocolate mixture into egg whites. Pour in small dessert cups or leave in mixing bowl. Chill.

Ellen Hansen

TRANSPLANTED DATE PUDDING

1 lb. dates, chopped or ground
1/2 cup nuts
1 box graham crackers (small box)
Marshmallows (small ones)
Cream or sweet milk

Serves 16.

Grind crackers to crumbs. Grind dates alternately with crackers. If you don't have a grinder, you can just mix the ingredients. (Be sure the dates are chopped small if they are not ground.) Add marshmallows and nuts, and mix with just enough cream (or sweet milk) to make it stick together. Roll and place it in the refrigerator. The secret lies in working it all together with as little milk as possible. Slice it 1/2" thick and serve with whipped cream and a cherry (or strawberry) on top.

Onis Gooden

Onis Gooden used to live on Fairview where the storms from the southwest had a bad habit of blowing her house off its raft. She's since moved to the calmer waters of Portage Bay. This pudding will keep for weeks in the refrigerator. It's good to serve when friends drop in, as well as for dessert.

Apricot Baba Au Rhum

4 cups stewed fresh apricots in heavy syrup
   or canned apricots (not nearly as tasty)
4 slices of Hovis (Canadian) bread about 3/4" thick
1/4 cup sugar (1/2 cup if canned apricots are used)
1 tsp. ground cinnamon
1/4 tsp. ground cloves
3 tsp. fresh grated ginger
2 T. grated orange peel
1 T. grated lemon peel
1/2 cup frozen orange juice, undiluted
6 oz. Jamaican dark rum (heavy dark rum is essential!)
Whipped cream or, if intimidated, yogurt
Fresh nutmeg

*C*learly the world's greatest dessert, this recipe was developed aboard the sailboat "Navita" during a summer cruise in Canadian waters. A 10 pound sack of apricots, on sale at a local fruit stand, couldn't be passed up. As a result, we ate this dessert until the sack was empty!

Makes four generous servings — scarcely enough for two hungry people.

Heat the stewed apricots in a saucepan with the sugar, cinnamon, ginger, cloves, orange peel, lemon peel and orange juice. Bring to a boil and simmer for five minutes. In a soup plate place a slice of Hovis bread and slowly pour over it 1 1/2 oz. of rum. (The reason for Hovis bread is that it is so glutinous that it doesn't disintegrate when the rum is poured on it. Someone should have a bread tasting party to identify a local whole wheat bread substitute.) Spoon out two tablespoons of the hot syrup on each slice of bread followed by one cup of the apricots. Top with yogurt or whipped cream and grated fresh nutmeg.

Art Hemenway

FLOATING PEARS PARISIENNE

4 or 5 whole fresh pears (any hard pear, like Bosc)
1 orange
1 lemon
1/2 cup white sugar
1 oz. unsweetened chocolate, grated
Ice cream or whipped cream

Poach pears until tender but still firm. Save pear juice. Squeeze juice from orange and lemon. Put rinds into food processor or fine blade of food chopper. Whir or chop until fine. Add 1/2 cup pear juice and reserve remainder. Puree until smooth but textured.

Pour sauce into a saucepan and cook until thick (about 15 or so minutes). Add additional pear juice if too thick. Add pear halves to sauce. Let stand a few hours or overnight.

Top individual servings with ice cream or whipped cream. Sprinkle with grated unsweetened chocolate. Garnish with orange and lemon zest.

Peg Stockley

This started out as an old family recipe entitled "Pears Parisienne" (I'm not sure why). When it followed us to our houseboat on Lake Union we adapted the name and also modernized the recipe for a food processor.

PORTAGE BAY BLACKBERRY GRUNT

Filling:
4 cups home-picked blackberries
1/3 cup sugar
2 T. flour
1/2 tsp. cinnamon
1/4 tsp. salt
1 tsp. vanilla extract
1 T. soft butter or margarine

Batter:
1/2 cup flour
1/2 cup sugar
1/2 tsp. baking powder
1/4 tsp. salt
2 T. soft butter or margarine
1 egg

Serves 6.

Mix all filling ingredients, put in baking pan or loaf pan, and dot with butter or margarine. Mix all batter ingredients and drop in 8 or 9 portions on blackberries.

Bake at 375 F. for 35 to 40 minutes and serve with vanilla ice cream.

Elaine Powell

*H*ere's a tip. Don't wash berries before storing them in the refrigerator. They'll keep longer.

OVER THE WAVES FRUIT TORTE

1 cup sugar
1/2 cup butter or margarine
2 eggs
1 cup flour
1 tsp. baking powder
1 dash salt
2 cups quartered fruit (plums, apricots, peaches, etc.)
2 T. sugar
1 tsp. cinnamon
1 tsp. lemon peel
1 tsp. lemon juice

Serves 6-8.

Butter a 10 inch baking dish.

Cream together 1 cup sugar and butter until fluffy, add eggs and beat well. Combine flour, baking powder and salt and add to mixture and beat at low speed. Spread in prepared pan.

Arrange fruit, skin side up, on crust. Combine sugar and cinnamon and sprinkle over fruit. Combine lemon peel and juice and sprinkle over fruit.

Bake at 350 F. for 50-60 minutes until done. Cool.

Bob Williams

Seattle, Washington

RASPBERRY TART

Crust:
1 cup flour
1/4 cup white sugar
1/4 cup frozen almonds
1 egg
1 tsp. vanilla or almond extract
2/3 stick frozen butter

Filling:
4 cups raspberries
1/4 cup sugar
Pinch nutmeg or cinnamon
1 tsp. grated lemon rind
1/4 cup flour

Whipped cream and a few fresh berries for decoration

Serves 6.

Place flour, sugar and frozen almonds in food processor and blend until texture is fine. In a small bowl, blend together egg and vanilla or almond extract and set aside. Cut frozen butter into small chunks. Turn on food processor and drop chunks of butter into chute until coarsely chopped into flour mixture. Turn on food processor again and pour egg mixture through chute and let run until mixture forms a moist ball of dough. Pat the dough onto the bottom and sides of an 8" springform pan.

Place all filling ingredients in a bowl and toss gently with a wooden spoon until blended, being careful not to squash raspberries too much. Spread filling into tart shell.

Bake in preheated 375 F. oven for 25 minutes (or until crust is browned). Serve warm or chilled with whipped cream and a few fresh berries as decoration.

Blair Robbins and Bob Burk

In the early 1970's, before the radical remodel boom had started, many houseboats were designed "shotgun" style -- you entered at one end of the house, usually through the kitchen, next came the living room, then the bedroom.

I went to a wedding shower on one of these old houseboats and, by the time most of the guests had arrived, the front porch was under water. We had to spread out to the other rooms to even the weight so we wouldn't swamp the house.

Houseboat Old-timer

LAZYBONES BLUEBERRY TART

Crust:
1 cup flour
2 T. sugar
1/2 cup soft butter
1 T. white vinegar

Filling:
4 cups blueberries
1/2 cup sugar
3 T. flour
1 tsp. cinnamon

Powdered sugar
Whipped cream

Serves 4-6

Crust: Work together with fingers the flour, sugar and butter. Add the vinegar. Push into tart pan (spring release pan). Filling: Mix sugar, flour and cinnamon. Add 3 cups blueberries and pour into crust. Bake at 400 F. for 30 minutes.

Add the other cup of blueberries while tart is still hot. When the tart is cool, sprinkle with powdered sugar. Serve with whipped cream.

Claire Tangvald

This is an easy, scrumptious tart for Fall blueberry picking season in the mountains, provided, of course, you don't eat them all before you get home!

STRAWBERRIES TO DIE FOR

1-2 pints strawberries, stems left on
Small bag of semi-sweet chocolate bits
1 tsp. vanilla
2 T. plain yogurt
Splash Cointreau, Drambuie, or some such liqueur

Wash strawberries, let dry well on towels or rack. Melt chocolate in top of double boiler over medium heat. This should take about 15 minutes. Stir in vanilla, yogurt and liqueur. Dip berries (about half only) into chocolate and set on wax paper placed on a plate. Do not let them touch each other. Refrigerate, then transfer to platter before serving.

Diane Pettengill from Ladies Poker Night

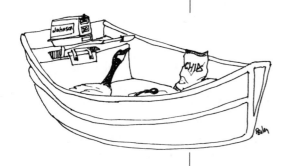

CHOCOLATE DECADENCE

Cake:
1 lb. semi-sweet chocolate
1/2 cup plus 2 T. butter
6 eggs
1 T. sugar
1 T. flour

Topping:
1 or 2 cups whipping cream
1 tsp. Vanilla extract
1/4 cup confectioners sugar

Raspberry Sauce:
2 cups (or 1 bag whole frozen) raspberries
Simple sugar (6 T. sugar + 3 T. water)

Serves 8.

Preheat oven to 425 F.

Prepare an 8" cake pan by lining the bottom with a circle of parchment paper (a brown paper bag works just fine too).

In a double boiler, melt the chocolate and butter. In a mixing bowl, combine the eggs and sugar and place in a hot water bath. Heat this mixture, stirring until warm (approx. 120 degrees). Using a mixer, whip the egg mixture at high speed until double in volume, about 10 minutes.

Gently fold flour into the egg mixture. Add chocolate mixture, fold in gently. Pour into the prepared cake pan. Bake 10 minutes (only the edges will be firm). Remove from oven and cool. Freeze overnight.

To remove cake, place it in a warm oven for a few minutes and then turn pan upside down over a plate. Remove parchment. Whip cream with vanilla and sugar to taste and ice cake.

Puree the raspberries in a blender or food processor. Bring sugar and water to a boil in a small saucepan to make a simple sugar. Add to pureed berries and mix. You can serve French style with the sauce on the plate or spoon sauce over cake.

Judy Shaw

My partner loves chocolate! I have tried many recipes and they were never "chocolatey" enough. Short of serving a Hershey Bar on a plate, this is it!

My husband loves chocolate. I had just purchased two packages of chocolate wafers to make a pie crust and the next day I noticed a package was missing. When I confronted him about the wafers he denied having eaten them. I didn't really believe him, but didn't pursue it. A couple of weeks later a friend and I were up late talking. About 3 a.m. we heard a rustle in the kitchen. Two raccoons were dragging the remaining box of chocolate wafers to a hole in the pantry floor and were in the process of making a clean get-away. The next morning I had to confess and apologize for doubting my husband's honesty, but that still leaves dozens of bags of chocolate chips unaccounted for!

Jann McFarland

FROZEN FRANGOS

1/2 lb. butter
2 cups sifted powdered sugar
4 squares unsweetened baking chocolate
4 eggs
2 tsp. vanilla
1 tsp. peppermint extract, rum or Kahlua

Melt chocolate in double boiler. Beat butter and sugar. Add melted chocolate. Then add the eggs one at a time as you continue mixing. Stir in vanilla and either peppermint, rum or Kahlua. Put into cupcake papers and freeze. About 1/2 hour prior to serving, remove from freezer.

Pam Goetz

SAM'S CHOCOLATE BOMB SUPERB

8 oz. semi-sweet chocolate
4 oz. sweetened chocolate
2/3 cup strong coffee
1 1/2 tsp. vanilla
8 T. sweet butter (1 stick)
2/3 cup walnuts
2 cups whipping cream
1 T. confectioner's sugar

Serves 8.

In double boiler over moderate heat, melt chocolates in the coffee. Add 1 tsp of the vanilla and let mixture cool 10 minutes. Meanwhile, barely melt the sweet butter, grind walnuts to a powder and mix together. Stir butter-walnut mixture into the cooled chocolate mixture. Beat 1 cup whipping cream until it peaks and fold carefully into the above.

Coat inside of a one-quart stainless steel mixing bowl (or whatever) with vegetable oil and pour mixture into it. Cover tightly with foil or plastic and leave in freezer for at least four hours. Remove from mold (dip briefly in warm water) and put on a plate. Store in freezer. Whip 1 cup of cream mixed with 1 T. of confectioner's sugar and 1/2 tsp. vanilla until stiff. Spread this over the frozen chocolate and return to freezer. Slice as a cake when ready to serve.

Helen Mitchell

DOCK PARTY PECAN SQUARES

Pastry shell:
2 sticks (1 cup) butter
1/2 cup sugar
1 egg
1/4 tsp. salt
Finely grated rind of 1 large lemon
3 cups sifted all-purpose flour

Pecan Topping:
2 sticks (1 cup) butter, cut in pieces
1/2 cup honey
1/4 cup granulated sugar
1 cup plus 2 T. dark brown sugar, firmly packed
1/4 cup heavy cream
20 oz. (5 cups) pecan halves

Makes about 4 dozen.

Adjust rack 1/3 up from bottom of oven and preheat to 375 F. Butter a 15 1/2" x 10 1/2" x 1" jelly-roll pan and place it in the freezer or refrigerator. (It's easier to spread this dough on a cold pan.)

In a large bowl of electric mixer cream the butter and sugar just to mix well. Beat in the egg, salt and lemon rind. Gradually add the flour and beat only until mixture is smooth and holds together.

Place mixture by large spoonfuls all over the bottom of the cold pan. With floured fingertips press firmly all over the bottom and the sides. There must not be any holes or thin spots in the bottom. Prick the bottom at 1/4 inch intervals with a fork. Chill in the freezer or refrigerator for about 10 minutes.

Bake 20 minutes until half baked and lightly colored around the edges. If dough puffs up while baking, reach in to prick it with a fork very slightly and gently. Remove from oven but do not turn off oven heat. Prepare topping.

In heavy 3-quart saucepan over moderately high heat, cook the butter and honey until butter is melted. Add both sugars and stir to dissolve. Bring to a boil and let boil without stirring for exactly 2 minutes.

Many docks have a 4th of July party because we have front row seats for the fireworks on Lake Union. There are parties to commemorate special historical events such as the signing of a lease or victory in a land-use battle. Births, weddings, work parties, a sunny day -- let's have a party! Imagine the "oohs" and "aahs" when a pan of these pecan squares shows up at your next get-together.

Without waiting, remove from heat and stir in heavy cream and pecans. Immediately spread the hot mixture evenly over the half-baked crust, spreading with the back of a wooden spoon to make as even as possible.

Bake in 375 F. oven with rack in same position for 25 minutes. Remove from oven and cool completely. Cut around sides to release. Cover with a cookie sheet. Invert and remove pan. (If pan doesn't lift off easily it is because some of the topping has run through to the bottom. If this has happened, bang the inverted pan sharply against the cookie sheet to release.)

Cover with a large rack or another cookie sheet and invert again right side up. Slide off onto a cutting board. With a long, heavy knife, cut into small squares, cutting down firmly with the full length of the blade, and wiping the blade frequently with a damp cloth.

M. Liz Crowell

PORTAGE BAY GRANOLA BARS

6 T. cooking oil
1 cup brown sugar
1 cup whole wheat flour
1 cup granola, any kind
4 eggs, beaten
2 cups brown sugar
1 1/2 tsp. vanilla
1/4 cup whole wheat flour
1 tsp. salt (optional)
1 tsp. baking powder
2 cups walnuts, chopped
2 cups sunflower seeds

Makes approximately 4 dozen.

Mix first four ingredients together well; press into ungreased 9" x 13" pan. Bake at 350 F. for 10 minutes.

While this is baking, beat together well, eggs, brown sugar and vanilla. Add flour, salt and baking powder; beat. Fold in sunflower seeds and walnuts.

When first mixture is done baking, pour the second mixture over it, spreading evenly. Return to oven and bake 25 minutes more. Cool before cutting into 1 1/2" squares.

Note: I have also added raisins, blueberries, almonds or other goodies to replace portions of the walnut/sunflower seeds for variations. A little cinnamon is also nice on top.

Peg Boley

S'MORE BARS

1 13 1/2 oz. box of graham cracker crumbs
1 cup flour (either graham or white)
1 tsp. baking powder
1 tsp. baking soda
3/4 tsp. salt
1 cup butter or margarine
1 1/8 cups white sugar
1 1/8 cups brown sugar
3 eggs
1 1/2 tsp. vanilla
2 7 oz. bars of chocolate (milk, semisweet, or both)
3/4 of a 10 oz. bag of large marshmallows
Chopped nuts (optional)

Makes about 5 dozen.

Sift together dry ingredients and set aside. Melt butter and pour into large bowl. Stir in white and brown sugar, beat until smooth. Add the eggs one at a time and beat. Stir in vanilla. Add 1/3 of dry mixture to wet mixture and beat until blended. Add the next 1/3 and beat; add the rest and mix until blended.

Lightly grease a broiling pan or pan of similar size (about 12" x 18" x 1 1/4"). Press 2/3 of the dough onto bottom and up sides. Break up the chocolate bars onto the dough. Add the marshmallows by pressing them on top of the chocolate. (I tear or cut them into 4ths because they seem to melt better than mini marshmallows). Sprinkle on chopped nuts if desired.

Press remaining dough on top, covering as much area as possible (a mottled effect). Bake at 325 F. for 20 minutes or until dough is done (I usually underbake a tad). Let cool before cutting into bars.

Elissa Kamins

I bake for a hobby, inventing something new every time, always changing and perfecting recipes. Usually something will spark an idea; a fruit coming into season, a friend's birthday dream cake, a new item in the grocery store, or just new combinations from stuff off my shelves at home.

Last summer I drove to Montana and visited some friends. We camped through Yellowstone, and every night planned on making S'mores and every night we never did. As I drove back to Washington, I decided to invent a S'more Bar I could send back to my friends in Big Sky Country -- something that would hold up through the mails and still be a tasty treat. After many alterations, this is the latest version.

Seattle, Washington

POLAR BEAR SCOTCHIES

1 cup butter
4 cups brown sugar
4 eggs
2 tsp. vanila
1/2 cup cream
4 cups flour
4 tsp. baking powder
1/2 tsp. salt
12 oz. semi-sweet real chocolate chips
1 1/2 cups walnuts

Makes 2 dozen.

Melt butter over low heat. Remove from heat and stir in brown sugar.
Add eggs and beat well. Stir in vanilla. Add dry ingredients and the
cream. Stir well. Add chocolate chips and nuts and mix throughout.
Spread in greased 15" x 10" x 1" pan (or thereabouts). Bake at 350 F.
for 25 minutes. Eat immediately with milk or beer.

Debra Boyer

2235 Fairview, heart of the Lake Union Polar Bear Club, started February 2, 1980. As years go by, it has been necessary to provide quick starters for the old engines. These will do it. There's enough sugar and fat in these scotchies to give a Scot a sense of humor.

AUNT SHIRLEY PROUDFOOT'S CHRISTMAS DATE SQUARES

Filling:
1 lb. dates (chopped)
Rind of 1 lemon, grated
Rind of 1 orange, grated
Juice of 1 lemon
Juice of 2 oranges
1/2 cup water
1 cup sugar

Crusts:
1 1/2 cups chopped walnuts
2 1/2 cups flour
2 1/4 cups oats
3/4 tsp. baking soda
1 1/2 cups brown sugar
1 cup melted butter

Makes 16 squares.

Mix filling ingredients in saucepan and cook thoroughly like a heavy applesauce. Set aside to cool.

Mix crust ingredients in bowl. Pack 1/2 crust mix in 8" x 8" pan. Add the cooled filling and spread over bottom crust. Pack remaining crust mix on top. Bake in center of oven at 350 F. for 35-45 minutes. Cool. Cut in 2" squares.

Mack Hopkins

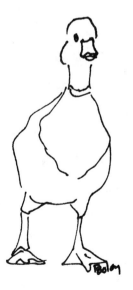

CHOCOLATE FROSTED RUMMAGE SALE COOKIES

For almost 10 years our dock held an annual rummage sale. The proceeds went to pay for our summer party, but the sale was almost as fun as the party! We sold Chili Dogs and Cookies, drank beer, and tried out the "stuff" everyone was selling. We usually ended up buying a neighbor's junk, then putting it back in the sale the next year. One year someone donated some little plastic bed pans. We put rope on them and tagged them as "Walk-on-the-Water" shoes — a hot item.

Cookies:
3 oz. unsweetened chocolate, melted
1/2 cup softened butter
1 cup sugar
1 egg
1 tsp. vanilla
1 1/4 cups sifted flour
1/4 tsp. salt
1 1/2 tsp. baking powder

Frosting:
2 oz. unsweetened chocolate
1/3 cup butter
2 to 3 cups powdered sugar
Pinch salt
Brewed coffee
Almond extract

Makes about 3-4 dozen cookies, depending on size.

Cookies: Preheat oven to 350 F. Cream butter and sugar until thick and light in color. Beat in egg and vanilla. Partially blend in chocolate. Sift together flour, salt, baking powder; add to chocolate mixture. Blend well. Drop by spoonfuls onto buttered cookie sheet. Bake 5 to 8 minutes. Cool.

Frosting: Melt chocolate and butter in saucepan over low heat. Add pinch of salt. Add 2 cups powdered sugar and 2 to 3 T. coffee. Continue to stir over low heat. Add more powdered sugar and coffee until desired consistency reached. (Warm frosting needs to be of a slightly thinner consistency.) Add 2 to 5 drops almond extract. Frost cookies.

Linda Knight

MOLASSES OATMEAL COOKIES

1 cup brown sugar
1/2 cup margarine
1 egg
1/2 cup molasses
2 cups flour
1 tsp. salt
1 1/2 tsp. baking soda
1/2 tsp. cinnamon
2 cups rolled oats
1/2 cup chopped nuts
1/2 cup seedless raisins or dates

Makes about 4 dozen small cookies.

Cream sugar and margarine. Add egg and molasses and beat well. Add dry ingredients and mix well. Stir in chopped nuts and raisins or dates. Drop batter from teaspoon onto greased cookie sheet and bake at 350 F. for 12-15 minutes.

Anna Brown

COUSIN MARTHA'S ALMOND COOKIES

1/2 cup butter
1/2 cup powdered sugar
1 cup ground almonds
3/4 cup sifted flour
1/2 tsp. salt
Candied cherries

Makes approximately 2 1/2 dozen cookies.

Mix ingredients except cherries. Shape into small balls and flatten out on ungreased baking sheet. Decorate with 1/2 candied cherry each. Bake at 350 F. for 8-10 minutes.

Mack Hopkins

MARIA OLMSTED'S SOUR CREAM COOKIES

1 cup shortening (margarine is best)
2 cups sugar
4 cups flour
1 cup sour cream
1 level tsp. baking soda, beaten in sour cream
2 eggs (not beaten)
1 tsp. vanilla
1/8 tsp nutmeg
1 tsp. salt

Makes 3-4 dozen.

By hand, cream sugar and shortening. Add eggs, sour cream, flour, salt, nutmeg and vanilla. Mix well. Drop onto cookie sheet and bake in 375 F. oven for about 12 minutes.

Hellen Nelson

This recipe is an old one from Anne LeVasseur's mother, Mrs. Olmsted. They're delicious!

FROSTY APPLE BITES

2 cups flour
1/2 tsp. baking soda
1/2 tsp. salt
1/4 tsp. nutmeg
1/4 cup butter
1 cup brown sugar, packed
1 egg
1 tsp. vanilla
2/3 cup evaporated milk
1 cup chopped walnuts
1 cup pared, chopped apples
1/2 cup semi-sweet chocolate morsels

Glaze:
2 cups sifted powdered sugar
3 T. melted butter
1 tsp. cinnamon
2-3 T. evaporated milk

Yields 4 1/2 dozen.

Sift together the flour, baking soda, salt and nutmeg and set aside.
Cream the butter, gradually adding the brown sugar. Blend in the egg
and vanilla. Beat well. Add the dry ingredients alternately with the
evaporated milk, beginning and ending with the dry ingredients, blending after each addition. Stir in the walnuts, apples and chocolate. Drop
by teaspoonfuls onto lightly greased cooked sheets. Bake at 375 F. for
12-15 minutes. When cool, frost with cinnamon glaze.

Glaze: Combine sugar, butter and cinnamon. Add the evaporated milk
a little at a time until spreading consistency.

Hazel Nigh

HELLEN'S OATMEAL COOKIES

2/3 to 1 cup shortening
2 cups brown sugar
2 eggs, beaten
1 1/2 cups flour
2 cups rolled oats
2 tsp. baking powder
1/2 tsp. salt
1 tsp. cinnamon
1 T. vinegar
1/2 cup raisins
1/2 cup nuts

Makes about 5 dozen.

Cream together sugar and shortening. Add eggs, then sifted dry ingredients, rolled oats, flavoring, nuts, and/or fruit. Drop from teaspoon onto greased baking sheets. Bake at 400 F. for 10 minutes.

Hellen Nelson

This recipe is from the Good Housekeeping Cookbook, 7th edition. The cookbook has had a history of traveling to Alaska in its spare time. My brother hired on a fish boat to Alaska and borrowed it. It took another trip while we were moored on the west side of Lake Union on a moorage of 35 houseboats that were all evicted in 1962 to make room for a "Boatell" for the World's Fair. One day a pleasure boat was docked nearby and it needed a cook for a charter to Alaska. Esther Carhart (later to lose her home in the Columbus Day storm and even later to become an early president of the Floating Homes Association) borrowed my cookbook and signed on the spot! So both the cookbook and the recipe have a houseboat history.

WAACO (Women's Attitude Adjustment Camp Out) began with 6 women from Oregon and Washington camping out 16 years ago. Now they meet twice a year somewhere between Oregon and Washington and at least 30 of them show up every time. For some it is loud and rowdy; for others it's quiet walks on the beach, but there are always interesting perspectives on getting through life female so most of us keep coming back. There is also lots of good food. Even the "junk food" is good. It will be obvious from the recipe that one of the WAACO's sells Tupperware. Every time I buy Tupperware it disappears. I'm beginning to think those "Tupperware friends" who coax you into attending those parties ("It'll be fun and you don't have to buy anything") (HA!), also employ gangs of "Tupperware burglars".

KAYAKER'S SNACK

1 box Crispix cereal
1 cup peanut butter
12 oz. bag chocolate chips
1 stick butter
1 box powdered sugar

Melt chocolate chips, peanut butter and butter in microwave. Stir into cereal in a Tupperware "fix-n-mix" bowl. Add one box powdered sugar. Seal and shake. Yum!!

Sheri Lockwood

Seattle, Washington

FROM BATHTUB GIN TO A FINE GLASS OF WINE

Beverages

SIPPING AFLOAT

By Tom Stockley

Most of us equate the imbibing of alcoholic beverages as sipping a cool glass of crisp chardonnay on the deck of our houseboat on a lovely summer's day. Perhaps a crawfish or two might accompany that classy wine as an appetizer.

But the history of drinking afloat wasn't always so polite and sedate. In fact, it was darn right rowdy. Prohibition ushered in an interesting and colorful chapter in the houseboats' history. It was an eventful period of rumrunners, high-speed chases across the lake and floating speakeasies which dispensed gin, gambling and (ahem) other worldly pleasures. It also gave rise to some legendary Lake Union characters.

Roy Olmstead, "king of the rumrunners," was one who had his speedy boats built at J.K. Farrow's boatyard on Portage Bay. They could outmaneuver any Coast Guard boat, but they were occasionally fired upon. While Lake Union Dry Dock kept the rum-chasers in good repair, smaller boatyards on Lake Union and Lake Washington took care of the victims (as documented in Howard Droker's great book, "Seattle's Unsinkable Houseboats").

Daniel Drygert was another. Born at the north shore of the lake in 1916, he was already transporting liquor around the lake's various speakeasies as a teenager. And there were plenty on the lake to service. Droker's book documents a number of gin joints all around the lake. Sometimes they were raided. "In April of 1926," writes Droker, "police arrested John Spring of 1613 Fairview East, after discovering 1,500 bottles of home-made beer and another 50 gallons brewing at his houseboat. Later that same month, a county deputy sheriff raided an empty houseboat on Westlake North and dumped 1,500 bottles of home brew into the lake.

Then there was the infamous four-masted ship — the William T. Lewis — which was moored in the lake that, according to the Seattle Times in 1926, "fell on evil days." "It was disclosed the once famous Glascow ship, moored in Lake Union for months, has been used as a floating brewery and moonshine distiller. . . . The raiding party used a rowboat as a means of transportation to the ship, arriving just in time to see the trio throw a five-gallon can of alcohol overboard. One shot

Tom Stockley has written the wine column for the Seattle Times for 20 years. He also writes for national publications on the subject of food and wine. Tom lives on a houseboat on Lake Union with his wife, Peggy, and assorted stray cats.

fired by Carrothers (the federal agent) halted the attempt to dump the liquor."A number of trapdoors in older houseboats still tell their story of those wilder days.

But, back to that frosty glass of chardonnay. Just think, you don't have to toss it overboard if you see the patrol boat coming along. Which brings me to the point of all this. We have a lot of parties on our dock (Tenas Chuck), mostly outdoors in the summer. And I have developed a list of wines that seem to work for potlucks when just about every flavor and texture shows up on the table. There are plenty of decent wines to serve that won't cost you an arm and a leg. Here are my suggestions for three different kinds of get-togethers:

CHEAP BUT GOOD

Try some of the magnum sized (1.5 liters) bottlings such as Sebastiani, M.G. Vallejo, Glen Ellen from California and Washington Hills, Allison Combs and Farron Ridge from Washington. Their chardonnays, sauvignon blancs, generic dry whites, blush wines and reds are all quite good for the price. I generally find that white and blush go first, so I shop with that in mind. Blush wines, not one of my favorites, do seem to compliment potlucks and are always popular. I always add a bottle or two of merlot or cabernet sauvignon for those of us who like a heartier wine with hamburgers and hot dogs.

CLASSIER BUT STILL AFFORDABLE

This is where you graduate into fifths with real corks. You may even want to use stemmed glasses (we're getting big-time now). I like chardonnays and sauvignon blancs by Estancia, Domaine St. George, Napa Ridge, Swan Cellars and Mondavi's Woodbridge Cellars. These same wineries also make decent cabernet sauvignon and some-times merlot. But I rely on Bel Arbors for many of my reds and, for a pinot noir, Mountain View. From the Northwest, there are a number of affordable labels on the market including Washington Hills, Covey Run, Columbia Crest and Zillah Oakes. If you want a step up in quality, reach for some of the wines by Hogue Cellars, Latah Creek, Columbia, Chateau Ste. Michelle or Stewart Vineyards. And don't forget some of the newer dry rieslings from the Northwest. They make great sipping wines at gatherings and go nicely with food.

PUTTIN' ON THE RITZ

My dockmates love champagne, especially when I provide it (just kidding folks). Seriously, we do like a bit of the bubbly around holiday parties and special occasions. Some of the Spanish sparklers are well made and affordable. I particularly like the Freixenet, Paul Cheneau, Castelblanch Brut Zero and Cordoniu. The Northwest has a good sparkler, Domaine Ste. Michelle's Champagne Brut, an excellent choice.

Seattle, Washington

One summer my neighbor, long-time dock resident and party queen, Rachel, built a large raft out of scavenged logs, Styrofoam and decking. An engine mount was added on one end and, voilà, a mobile deck! Many a warm evening we loaded the deck chairs, gas barbecue, ice chest and dining room table aboard and headed for the middle of the lake for our favorite activities—eating, drinking, swimming and laughing. One evening a very large, brand-spanking-new motor yacht at least 4 stories high approached our raft. A very red-faced, flustered skipper leaned out the pilothouse window and yelled, "Darn you guys! I spent a quarter million dollars on this boat and you're having more fun!"

EASY GIN FIZZES FOR A CROWD

1 12 oz. can orange juice
3 12 oz. cans water
1 6 oz. can lemonade (no water)
8 T. sugar
Gin
Half & half

Each blender full serves 5-6.

Mix orange juice, water, lemonade and sugar in large pitcher. Then measure into blender one 12 oz. can of mixture, 2/3-3/4 of a 12 oz. can of gin, and one 12 oz. can of half & half. Blend well and pour into empty half gallon milk carton and store in refrigerator overnight, or freeze if not to be used the next day. Mixture will keep frozen for several months.

To serve: fill blender 1/3 to 1/2 full of ice, add fizz mixture (shake before pouring) and blend.

Marty Alexander

BASTILLE DAY SANGRIA

Crate of ripe peaches
5 fifths cheap sherry
8 gallons cheap white chablis
1 box powdered sugar
3-4 people with paring knives

Serves 200.

The beauty of this recipe is that you don't have to peel the peaches, just slice them up and dump into a large container, even a small garbage pail (clean, hopefully). Add the sherry and sugar to taste. Stir, taste a lot and let sit overnight, covered. Right before you serve the sangria, put a block of ice in your serving container and scoop some of the peaches and sherry over the ice and pour white wine over that. Mix and taste. Add more peaches or wine to suit your taste.

The 2025 Pigroast Pit Crew

*A*fter putting the pig into the ground Friday night, we all grab a quick bite to eat and then assemble on someone's deck to make the sangria for the luau. The peaches sort of ferment in the sherry giving this punch a real punch...a lot of guests have eaten too many peaches!

SNAG-RIA

Full bottle Asti Spumante (I prefer champagne)
1/2 bottle Soave Bolla
1/2 cup brandy
1/2 cup sherry
2 to 3 oranges and some of the peel
1/2 fresh lemon

Serves 4-6.

Sugar rims of glasses. Mix all ingredients in large pitcher. Dump in orange chunks and peel. Squeeze in lemon juice. Smash fruit around in pitcher and stir. Fill pitcher with ice.

Marty Gardner

*S*tolen from an Italian restaurant

in Boston

LAKE UNION SMASHES

1 can frozen "Five Alive" juice
1 bottle of rum (dark rum is best)
Coconut flavoring (in the form of coconut rum,
    coconut extract, or coconut syrup)
Fresh lemons, limes or oranges for garnish

Make the juice in a pitcher. Add as much rum as you care to consume.
Add a dash of coconut flavoring (enough so you taste the coconut but it
does not overpower the flavor of the juice — you'll have to keep tasting
to know just how much you need). Add ice cubes and serve with slices
of lemon, lime, orange, or all three.

Marty Alexander

This recipe is adapted from that Bahamian favorite, the Goombay Smash. In the islands they use a mixture of fresh fruit juices, but I've found that "Five Alive" juice does the trick. This summer cooler tastes so good you'll forget that it's alcoholic — so watch out!

One year when we were aboard Art's boat, Navita, for a New Year's cruise to Port Ludlow with 10 or so people aboard, someone left Art's rum keg running (full of 151 proof). It dripped down onto the French bread supply for the weekend. We were forced to eat rum-soaked bread. (I believe that's the year we went aground too.) As a result we all had scurvy by the time we returned ashore — because we had not had our lime with our rum ration!

Anon. crew member

SCURVY PREVENTER

1 1/2 oz. Jamaican rum (Bacardi is worthless)
1/2 oz. Rose's Lime juice

Pour over large ice cubes.

Art Hemenway

SOUTHWIND-CHILL-REMOVER(HOT BUTTERED RUM MIX)

1 quart vanilla ice cream
1 lb. butter
1 lb. brown sugar
1 lb. powdered sugar
1 tsp. cinnamon
Rum
Nutmeg

Makes about 1 1/2 qts. of mix.

Put ice cream in a large bowl. Using a hand mixer, do not beat, but stir in each of the rest of ingredients one at a time. Batter can be stored for weeks in refrigerator or kept in freezer. Put heaping tablespoon (or two) in cup, add rum and hot water, stir, top with sprinkle of nutmeg.

Barbara and Dave Lefebvre

It is not unheard of for houseboats to break loose from their moorings in a big wind storm. Everyone on the dock rallies to help, holding ropes and trying to "rein in" the loose house before it hits other houses, and breaks electrical, telephone, TV cable and sewer lines. In the "Inauguration Day Windstorm" of 1993, many houseboats broke loose from their docks and the few people on each dock who were not at work were left to tie them back up.

KAYAK CAROLER'S DEMISE

*T*his is a drink to serve before and

after a Christmas canoe/kayak

caroling party. It helps build the

courage we need to go on singing

in the face of people threatening to

pour their eggnogs on us. It's also a

great warmer upper after the

adventure. (Lucky for us, people

are usually partying so loudly, they

can't hear us!)

Ingredients:
1 pot of freshly brewed (strong) coffee
1 cup of whipping cream (heavy cream, no sugar added)
Favorite bourbon, 1 oz. each glass
Amaretto, 1/2 oz. each glass (optional)
Sugar cubes, 2 each glass

Equipment:
Brandy glasses: If you don't have brandy glasses, use glasses that are short and wider at the bottom than at the top. You do not want a glass that is so large that the drink will cool before you finish it.
Blender: Do not use a mix master. The cream is prepared by blending, not whipping.
Two spoons
Shot glasses

Fill glasses with hot tap water. Pour whipping cream into the blender. Pour water out of the glasses after 2 minutes and quickly add 1 oz. of bourbon and 1/2 oz. of Amaretto. Quickly add coffee, leaving 1/2 inch for cream. Add 2 sugar cubes and stir.

Blend the cream (with flash blend) for 3 to 4 seconds. DO NOT OVER BLEND!! The cream should be only slightly thickened, with a light foam. BE CAREFUL!!

Place a spoon over the glass, with the bottom of the spoon just touching the coffee. Pour the cream slowly into the spoon, letting it flow onto (not into) the coffee.

YOU HAVE JUST MADE A PERFECT CREAMED BOURBON (& AMARETTO) COFFEE.

Sammie Pullen

THE BEST HOLIDAY EGGNOG

12 eggs separated
1/2 cup sugar
1 cup brandy, rye, whiskey or bourbon
1 cup rum
3 cups milk or half & half
1 cup cream, whipped but not too stiff
Nutmeg

Makes one large punchbowl full.

Beat egg yolks until thick and lemon colored. Gradually beat in sugar. Then gradually stir in booze. Cover and chill (a couple of hours at least, longer or overnight is better). Just before serving, stir in milk; then fold in stiffly beaten egg whites and whipped cream. Sprinkle with nutmeg.

Marty Alexander

I always serve this eggnog at my annual "caroling kayakers" Christmas party. Each year a local kayak rental business organizes three or four nights of caroling on the lake. Hearty souls actually pay to go out in the absolute worst weather and join in a group of 20 or 30 kayaks and paddle around the lake to prearranged houseboats to sing carols with us. Santa Claus, with long white beard and booming baritone voice, leads the singing, and the group is often joined by eight reindeer, complete with blinking antlers, rowing a shell. This is my very favorite party of the year, although the weather is usually so cold and blustery I have to drag my guests out on to the deck to sing along with the kayakers.

LAKE UNION CREAM LIQUEUR

This is good for a pick-me-up before entering the Duck Dodge race or for watching the Christmas Boats.

1 can (8-oz.) Eagle Brand condensed milk
1 1/2 cups half & half
12 oz. Canadian whiskey
1 T. Hershey's cocoa
1 1/2 T. instant coffee
2 eggs

Makes about 1 quart.

Mix in blender on high speed. (Watch out for foam!) Chill well. Enjoy!

Jim Burks

BOATER'S FOG

Fill a blender 3/4 full of vanilla ice cream. Add 1 cup whiskey and 1 cup cold strong coffee. Blend it. Yum!

Makes 4 large cups.

Huntley Holland-Olson

When asked to bring her favorite drink recipe to our Opening Boating Day party, our friend Caren Toney introduced us to this fabulous concoction. Among many other offerings, it was the most popular. It's now our Official Boating Day Drink, so we can toast the first day of boating season with CLASS (for at least the first 3 glasses).

Seattle, Washington

ORANGE JUBILEE

1 can (6 oz.) frozen orange juice concentrate
1 cup milk
1 cup water
1/4 cup sugar
1 tsp. vanilla
10 ice cubes

Makes 5 cups.

In blender, combine all ingredients. Process until ice cubes are crushed.

June Fauchald

Swedish "Glögg"

2 4-liter jugs of cheap, heavy red wine
1 3-liter jug of cheap port
1 bottle vodka
6-8 medium whole cinnamon sticks
1 scant tsp. whole green (or white) cardamom seeds (remove
    soft outer shells)
1 T. dried orange peel
10 whole cloves
1-2 T. sliced fresh ginger root
1 1/2 cups sugar
Almonds
Raisins

Initial Batch: Consume one of the 4-liter jugs of red wine (or you may pour the contents into some other container for later use). Into the empty jug put the cinnamon sticks, cardamom seeds, orange peel, cloves and ginger root. Pour enough vodka into the jug to barely cover the spices. Let it sit for a week, shaking occasionally.

Pour sugar into the container and add port to fill about 1/4 of the jug. Fill remainder of jug with heavy red wine.

To serve, pour glögg through a strainer into a pot (preferably glass) and heat on the stove. Put 3 whole almonds and 1/2 tsp. raisins into each cup and fill with glögg.

Subsequent Batches: Don't throw away the empty jug or try to remove the spices remaining on the bottom. Just add half as much spices as in the initial batch, pour some vodka on top of them and let sit for a week. Then add sugar, port and wine as described above. The glögg gets better and better with each batch!

Robert af Sandeberg

This is a traditional Swedish Christmas brew to warm your heart and tummy on cold winter days. The Mallard Cove drinking season is extended from the beginning of November to the end of February — or whenever the mood calls for it.

This recipe was given to me by a couple who lived on a houseboat back in the days when the community was a haven for Bohemian types and radicals. He was a longshoreman and both were very active in the labor union movement in Seattle. My friends and I used this recipe back when we didn't have much money for entertainment. In fact, to make it really cheaply, we had a medical student friend snag some lab alcohol (not the poison kind) to use in place of the vodka. I don't suggest doing that — it will knock you flat in no time at all!

LONGSHOREMAN'S PUNCH

1 gallon white or rosé wine
2 bottles soda water
1 fifth of vodka
1 quart of very strong black tea
6 oz. can frozen orange juice (with water added)
12 oz. can frozen lemonade (concentrate only)
Fresh fruit slices

Makes 2 1/3 gallons.

Mix all ingredients in large serving bowl.

Marty Alexander

RAMOS FIZZ

3 egg whites
3 or 4 ice cubes
1 cup Half & Half
6 heaping tsp. powdered sugar
3 jiggers lemon juice
1 jigger lime juice
6 jiggers gin
Soda water
Orange Flower Water

Serves 4

Blend all but soda and Orange Flower Water at high speed until ice is melted and mixture is frothy. Pour in glasses and top with 1/2 inch of soda water. Stir and splash with Orange Flower Water.

Jim Knight

A great morning drink for Christmas, New Years, Ground Hog's Day or other special occasions. It is a tradition to serve these drinks at the Knights' houseboat on Christmas Day when neighbors and "land" guests drop in for a Fizz or two throughout the day.

Seattle, Washington

One summer while cruising up north on our sailboat, we left Ganges Harbor and headed for Dodd Narrows and Nanaimo. Our ice supply had dwindled down to nothing. Somewhere along the way I came across an empty 5 liter wine box. Looking at the foil liner, and with ice on my mind, I figured that if I filled it with water and froze it I would have homemade block ice. It worked! Water frozen in these heavy foil bags will not leak out as it melts (there is some sweating) — a plus in any ice chest, and it lasts longer than store-bought ice. As it melts, it provides additional fresh ice water for that "cool one".

MARTY'S (WINE) BOX OF TRICKS

1 5 liter box of wine

Serves many purposes.

Drink the wine. Remove plastic spigot from foil liner (you may need pliers for this). Rinse liner. Fill empty liner with water, 3/4 full. Replace spigot and place in freezer until frozen solid. You may want to put water-filled foil back into its original box before freezing as this will give you a handy carrying container. For cooling efficiency, remove the frozen block from box before using.

Other possibilities (no foiling!):

- Forgot your pillow? Inflate foil liner. It'll never replace your goose down pillow but it's better than a coil of rope!

- Fill foil liner with hot (not boiling) water and you have an instant hot water bottle.

- Put ice chips and cold water in liner for an ice pack.

- Fill liner with fruit juice and freeze to take along on camping or kayak trip.

- Inflate liner and decorate with stickers for a quickie balloon.

Marty Gardner

Seattle, Washington

Floating Kitchens

Floating Homes Association, 2329 Fairview Avenue East., Seattle, WA 98102

Name: _____

Address: _____

City _____ State _____ Zip _____

Please send me _____ copies of Floating Kitchens at $14.95 per copy   _____

Washington residents add 8.2% sales tax at $1.23 per copy   _____

Shipping and handling at $2.00 per copy   _____

TOTAL ENCLOSED   _____

Please make check payable to Floating Homes Association and mail to above address.

- -

Floating Kitchens

Floating Homes Association, 2329 Fairview Avenue East., Seattle, WA 98102

Name: _____

Address: _____

City _____ State _____ Zip _____

Please send me _____ copies of Floating Kitchens at $14.95 per copy   _____

Washington residents add 8.2% sales tax at $1.23 per copy   _____

Shipping and handling at $2.00 per copy   _____

TOTAL ENCLOSED   _____

Please make check payable to Floating Homes Association and mail to above address.